Easy Grilling & Simple Smoking

with the

BBQ Queens

Easy Grilling & Simple Smoking

with the

BBQ Queens

Sauces, Rubs, Menus, BBQ Tips & More

by

Karen Adler & Judith Fertig
with Dee Barwick

PIG OUT PUBLICATIONS, INC.

First printing June 1997
Previously published as *Que Queens – Easy Grilling & Simple Smoking*

Copyright © 1997, 2001 by Pig Out Publications, Inc.
Cover Photo: Courtesy of the National Pork Producers Council
Cover photo recipes on pages 71 and 72
Cover design: Premila Borchardt
Text design: Jim Langford
Editor: Dee Barwick

Printed in the United States of America
ISBN 0-925175-26-9

10 9 8 7 6 5 4 3 2 1 01 02 03 04 05 06

Pig Out Publications, Inc., specializes in publishing and distributing barbecue and
grilling cookbooks. For corporate sales and special orders, or to receive a wholesale
catalog contact the publisher:

Pig Out Publications, Inc.
4245 Walnut Street, Kansas City, Missouri 64111
Phone: 816-531-3119
Fax: 816-531-6113

Consumer catalog offers over 200 barbecue and grilling titles at:
www.pigoutpublications.com

CONTENTS

PREFACE

The word "barbecue" means so many things. It means quick-grilling and slow-smoking. A barbecue may be a dinner of sophisticated flavors from the Southwest or a delicious down-home rib feast. If impromptu, it may be a pot luck. But whatever the menu, it brings people—friends and family—together for conversation, good food, and fun.

So, too, has this cookbook collaboration of authors and project coordinator, Dee Barwick, been fun. Her attention to creating the overall concept of the book and carrying it out to the smallest detail was a steady, kindly and tenacious triumph. We give our heartfelt thanks.

So what's the story? Who are the BBQ Queens, also known as the Que Queens? They are a group of women who share a love of good food, great friendship, and pride in their community. The Queens came together as an organization in response to a challenge! Someone, who shall remain nameless, declared that men were better barbecuers than women! Those are fighting words! So, we banned together to protect our culinary reputations, and those of womankind in general. In the process we raise funds and collect food for charity. *Love Potion for the Swine* is our own unique barbecue sauce, bottled to sell especially at charity events, compliments of BBQ Queen Karen Putman. Thanks to all the BBQ Queens: Karen Adler, Beckie Baker, Dee Barwick, Janeyce Michel-Cupito, Judith Fertig, Kathy Jones, Ronna Keck, Bobbi Marks, Karen Putman, Kathy Smith, Jean Tamburello, Lou Jane Temple, Bunny Tuttle, and Carolyn Wells.

A special tribute goes to Mary Ann Duckers for her excellent proofreading, delicious dessert recipe, and unflappable support. Thanks also to recipe contributors Richie Cusick and Joan Johnson. We dub these three women Honorary BBQ Queens along with Linda Ray of Family Features, whose talents delivered a beautifully typeset book.

BARBECUE BASICS

GRILLING

Grilling is defined as cooking over a direct heat source. The kind of grill you choose is determined by the space you have, the kind of fuel you want to use, the amount of cooking surface you need, and how much money you want to spend. The fuel choices are gas, electric, and charcoal/hardwood. Gas and electric grills are quick to start and easy to clean. When grilling on a gas or electric grill, follow the manufacturer's directions. Charcoal grills come in all sizes and shapes, with or without covers. The most popular grill "rig" for home use is the kettle-shaped grill.

SMOKING

Smoking is defined as the art of cooking indirectly over a low temperature wood fire slowly. There are gas, charcoal and electric smokers. Some are manufactured as water smokers, some are not. Smokers range in size from the compact bullet-shaped water smokers to trailer-sized rigs with hitches. Gas and electric grills can attain smoke by using a wood box and placing water-soaked wood in the box and placing the box close to the heat source. Aluminum foil can also be used to enclose soaked wood chips in a closed foil packet with a few holes poked on the top of the packet to release the smoke. The charcoal units can use hard wood lump charcoal as a base or charcoal briquettes with soaked wood chunks added.

THE FIRE, GRILLING TEMPERATURES, AND TIME

Charcoal fires can be started in any of several safe, ecologically sound ways. The charcoal is always mounded onto the lower fire grate of the grill except when using a charcoal chimney. When the fire is hot, spread the coals out in an even layer on the fire grate. This is the direct cooking area. The following items will aid you in easy fire starting:

The *charcoal chimney* is a straight, upright cylindrical metal canister. Fill the chimney with approximately 15-20 briquettes. Place it on a nonflammable surface, such as concrete or the top of the grill, and put crumpled paper in the bottom. Light the paper. After about 15 minutes, the coals will be hot. Empty the coals onto the lower fire rack of the grill.

The *electric starter* is the easiest way to start a fire. You'll probably need an outdoor electrical outlet or extension cord. Place the coil on the lower rack of the grill and stack charcoal on top of it. Plug it in and the fire will start in about 10 minutes. Remove the coil and let the starter cool on a nonflammable surface, out of the reach of children and pets.

Solid starters are compressed wood blocks or sticks treated with flammable substances, such as paraffin. They are easy to ignite and don't give off a chemical odor. Two or three will easily light the charcoal; set them on top of or beside the briquettes and ignite.

Grill directly over hot to medium-hot fires, depending on the distance your grill rack sits from the fire. The fire is ready when the flame has subsided and the coals are glowing red and just beginning to ash over. You can recognize a medium-hot fire when the coals are no longer red, but ashen. Another test to gauge the temperature is to hold your hand 5 inches above the heat source. If you can only hold it there for about 2 seconds, your fire is hot; 3 to 4 seconds is a medium hot fire, and 5 to 6 seconds is a low fire. Make sure that the grill rack is clean and lightly brushed with vegetable oil to prevent sticking.

Estimating cooking times is a challenge, because the time required to cook a meat varies due to the heat of the fire, the type of coals used, and the distance your heat source is from the grill. Use the suggested cooking times given in each recipe. A meat thermometer will be your ally with the safe internal meat temperatures printed on the thermometer.

THE ESSENTIAL UTENSILS

Several basic tools make grilling and smoking easier. A barbecue and grill shop or a restaurant supply store will be a good source for finding the items listed, and professional utensils are superior in quality and durability. Long handles are preferable on everything, to keep you a safe distance from the fire.

A stiff *wire brush* with a scraper makes cleaning the grill a simple job (tackle this while the grill is still warm).

Use a natural-bristled *basting brush* to brush oil on the grill to prevent sticking and get a separate brush for basting foods during cooking.

Heat resistant mitts offer the best hand protection, especially when you need to touch any hot metals during the grilling process.

Long-handled, spring-loaded *tongs* are easier to use than the scissors type. They are great for turning chicken pieces, steaks, vegetables, skewers and the like.

Keep a *spray bottle* filled with water by the grill to douse flare-ups. A garden hose within quick reaching distance can substitute, but make sure the water is turned on!

A long, wooden-handled offset *spatula* with a 5-to 6-inch blade is helpful for turning delicate items like ground meat burgers and fish fillets. Grease it well to avoid sticking.

Thermometers make guess work unnecessary. You'll need a grill thermometer to place inside the cooker for gauging the cooker's temperature and a meat thermometer to insert into the meat that you're cooking for an internal temperature.

WOODS

Smoke flavor comes from adding woods such as mesquite, hickory, oak, maple, pecan, alder and fruit woods like cherry, apple, pear, and grapevines to your cooking fire. Soaked woody herb stalks added to the grill fire offer another means of flavor enhancement. The heavenly odor in your backyard and flavor to your foods is your reward. Hardwoods like mesquite and oak burn hot. Wood chips, shavings, and sawdust are best for quick grilling. Soak them for about 30 minutes prior to grilling or keep a plastic container filled with wood chips in water. Throw a handful on the fire and if you want more smoke flavor while you're grilling, simply close the lid for a few minutes. Compressed wood pellets or larger chunks of wood are better for slow-smoking. Wood logs are often used in big rig smokers used by professional cooks, caterers, and barbecue competitors.

THE BASIC BARBECUE PANTRY

Stocking the outdoor cook's pantry is a wonderful way to save time. Your preferences in food will dictate the items you'll keep on hand and, as you experiment with new barbecue "styles," they may become more exotic. So we start here with the most essential pantry items.

Basic seasoning choices are: assorted peppers and salts like freshly ground black, red, and white pepper; pepper blends such as lemon pepper or seasoned pepper; preferred salts are sea and kosher salt, flavored salts are garlic, onion, and celery; plus garlic and onion powders. Chilies to stock include chili powder, paprika, red pepper, and red pepper flakes. Brown and white sugar plus honey are good sweeteners to have on hand always.

Dried herbs can be a selection of your favorites like: basil, oregano, parsley, rosemary, tarragon, sage, and thyme. Spices to include are dry mustard, ginger, cinnamon, cloves (whole and ground), coriander, and cumin.

Basic vinegars and oils to add to the pantry are: distilled white vinegar, cider vinegar, vegetable, canola, olive, and/or peanut oil. Fancy up the vinegar pantry with white, red, and rice wine vinegars. Upscale your oil selections with sesame, walnut, and garlic oils or make your own (page 9).

Condiments include bottled barbecue sauces, mustards, ketchup, soy sauce, Worcestershire, hot sauces, liquors, liqueurs, and fruit juices. Store bought marinades, grill seasonings, fruit jellies, preserves, chutneys, relishes, and salsas are convenient options and are available in grocery and gourmet stores.

BONE APPETIT

Secret Potions from the Queens' Cupboard

SECRET POTIONS FROM
THE QUEENS' CUPBOARD

RUBS

To penetrate meat for a deeper flavor and a juice-sealing crust, a combination of herbs and spices (called a rub) is pressed into surface of the food. For maximum taste, the rub should be applied at least an hour before cooking. Experiment with your own favorite combinations, use a prepared herb/spice mixture or try some of our favorite rub recipes, such as the *Que Queens' All-Purpose Rub*.

MOPS & MORE

Mops and bastes provide moisture and flavor when applied to foods that are cooking slowly over a low fire. They can be as simple as coffee or cola administered to the meat with a small dish mop, or as fancy as an herb infused baste brushed on with a new paintbrush. You can also use mops or bastes as a marinade to flavor the meat before cooking, then baste while smoking or grilling.

SAUCES & SUCH

Sauces, salsas, and chutneys are colorful condiments to serve with smoked or grilled foods as flavor complements. For a really royal treatment, create your own special blends to serve your guests or give as gifts.

OILS

Flavored or infused oils are easy to concoct and fun to use. Experiment with favorite herbs and develop your own "signature" blend. Use to replace any oil suggested in recipes for bastes, marinades, salsas, or salad dressings.

BUTTERS

Compound butters add a finishing touch to grilled or smoked entrees and an extra delicious jolt of flavor. Match the flavored butter to the meat, fish, poultry, or vegetable you want to highlight. Several of our favorite butter mixtures are included here. We hope they'll inspire you to create more!

THE QUE QUEENS' ALL-PURPOSE RUB

1/2 cup black pepper
1/2 cup paprika
1/4 cup garlic powder
1/4 cup onion salt
3 tablespoons dry mustard
3 tablespoons celery seed
3 tablespoons chili powder

Combine all ingredients and store in a glass jar. Rub into any kind of meat prior to cooking. *Makes 2 cups.*

THE QUE QUEENS' BLUE RIBBON RIB RUB

1 cup paprika
1/2 cup lemon pepper
1/2 cup black pepper
1/4 cup garlic salt
1/4 cup chili powder
1/2 cup brown sugar, packed

Combine all ingredients and store in a glass jar. Rub into ribs prior to cooking. *Makes 3 cups.*

AROMATIC HERB RUB

1/4 cup dried lemon peel
4 tablespoons dried basil
4 tablespoons dried tarragon
1 tablespoon garlic powder
1/2 tablespoon black pepper
1 teaspoon sea salt

Combine all ingredients and store in a glass jar. Rub into poultry or seafood before cooking. *Makes about 1/2 cup.*

SPICY BLACKENED SEASONING

4 tablespoons lemon pepper
2 tablespoons paprika
2 teaspoons white pepper
2 teaspoons dried parsley flakes
2 teaspoons garlic powder
1 teaspoon ground red pepper

Combine all ingredients and store in a glass jar. Rub into seafood or steaks before grilling quickly over very high heat for best results. *Makes about 1/2 cup.*

CITRUS SEAFOOD RUB

3 tablespoons dried ground lemon peel
3 tablespoons dried ground orange peel
3 tablespoons ground red peppercorns

Combine all ingredients and store in a glass jar. Sprinkle on shrimp, scallops and other seafood before grilling. *Makes about 1/2 cup.*

ROSEMARY RUB

3 tablespoons dried rosemary
3 tablespoons dried oregano
2 teaspoons lemon pepper
1 teaspoon garlic powder

Combine all ingredients and store in a glass jar. Rub into meat before grilling. Perfect for lamb. *Makes about 1/2 cup.*

BREW-PUB BASTE

1/2 cup oil
1 bottle of micro-brewed beer (ale or lager)
1/4 cup minced onion
Zest of 1 lemon
3 tablespoons sugar
1 tablespoon salt
1 teaspoon ground cloves

Combine all ingredients and store in a glass jar. Shake before using. Use as a baste or marinade. Excellent with game. *Makes about 2 cups.*

JAVA MARINADE AND BASTE

1 cup strong coffee
1/2 cup cider vinegar
1 tablespoon oil
1/4 cup chopped onion
3/4 cup brown sugar, packed
1 teaspoon dry mustard

Combine all ingredients and store in a glass jar. Use to baste or marinate poultry, pork, or beef. *Makes about 2 cups.*

MARGARITA MOP

1/2 cup cider vinegar
1/2 cup margarita mix
1/2 cup peanut oil
1 tablespoon spicy mustard
1/4 teaspoon ground red pepper

Combine all ingredients and store in a glass jar. Use to marinate or baste poultry or seafood. *Makes 1-1/2 cups.*

THE QUEENS' ALL-PURPOSE MOP AND MARINADE

2 cups spicy barbecue sauce
1 cup vegetable oil
1 cup cider vinegar

Combine all ingredients and store in a glass container. Use to marinate or baste pork, beef, or game. *Makes 4 cups.*

ROYAL JELLY

4 pickled peaches, pitted
6–10 cloves roasted garlic
1 cup orange juice
1/2 cup juice from a jar of pickled peaches
1/2 cup apple cider vinegar
4 ounces honey mustard
4 ounces yellow mustard
1/2 cup honey
1/2 cup tomato ketchup
1/8 cup hot sauce
1 tablespoon dry mustard
1 teaspoon white pepper
1 teaspoon kosher salt

Combine peaches and garlic in food processor and puree. Add this puree mix to all other ingredients in a large, heavy pan. Simmer for about 25 minutes, stirring often with a wooden spoon. The mixture will thicken and turn a light golden-orange color. Brush on meat during the last 5 to 10 minutes of cooking. *Makes about 3 cups.*

This very special recipe, which can be used as both a baste and a sauce, appears in the culinary mystery novel "Revenge of the Barbecue Queens," by Lou Jane Temple, our fellow Queen. Thanks, Lou Jane!

ASIAN GRILL MARINADE

1/4 cup soy sauce
1/4 cup rice wine vinegar
2 tablespoons peanut oil
2 tablespoons brown sugar
1 teaspoon freshly grated ginger
1 teaspoon toasted sesame oil

Combine ingredients. Excellent all-purpose marinade. *Makes about 3/4 cup.*

SMOKED CORN RELISH

3 cups smoked or roasted kernel corn
1 red onion, chopped
2 small jalapeno peppers, seeded and minced
4 cloves garlic, minced
2 tablespoons red pepper flakes
2 tablespoons dried leaf thyme
2 tablespoons chopped parsley
1/2 cup olive oil
1-1/2 cups white wine vinegar
1/2 cup sugar

Bring ingredients to boil, stirring often. Cool, bottle; refrigerate up to a week. *Makes 6 cups.*

APRICOT-PLUM SAUCE

2 cups plum jelly or jam
1 cup apricot preserves
2 teaspoons white vinegar
2 teaspoons sugar

Combine ingredients in food processor. Serve with poultry. *Makes 3 cups.*

PROVENCAL SALSA

1 (6-ounce) can black olives
1/2 cup chopped green olives
1 large tomato, chopped
1 tablespoon capers
2 tablespoons olive oil
2 tablespoons balsamic vinegar
1/2 teaspoon red pepper flakes

Combine all ingredients and let flavors blend. *Makes about 2 cups.*

FRESH PEACH CHUTNEY

3 cups chopped, peeled peaches, fresh or frozen
1/2 cup packed brown sugar
1/2 cup dried cherries or cranberries
1/2 cup chopped red onion
1/3 cup cider vinegar
1 teaspoon grated fresh ginger
1 clove garlic, minced

Combine all of the ingredients and chill. *Makes about 5 cups.*

SWEET & HOT MARMALADE CHUTNEY

2 cups chopped red onion
1/2 cup chopped dried apricots
1/2 cup orange marmalade
2 tablespoons white wine
2 tablespoons white wine vinegar
1/4 teaspoon ground white pepper
1/8 teaspoon dried red pepper flakes

Combine all ingredients in a glass bowl. Refrigerate overnight. *Makes about 3 cups.*

PUREED HERBAL OIL

1 cup extra virgin olive oil or canola oil
1/2 cup non-woody herbs
(parsley, cilantro, basil, tarragon, orange mint, lemon balm, etc.)

Use one type of herb or a combination. Put herb(s) and oil into food processor. Process until herbs are pureed. (Strain the mixture through a fine sieve to achieve a clear oil.) Pour flavored oil into a glass bottle and keep covered. *Makes 1 cup.*

GARLIC OIL

1 cup extra virgin olive oil or canola oil
6 to 8 large cloves garlic

Using a large chef's knife, smash the garlic on a wooden cutting board. Peel, but don't chop the garlic. Put the garlic and the oil in a heavy-bottomed saucepan and heat gently for about 25 minutes. Don't allow garlic to brown. Let the oil cool, then strain out garlic (which can be used in other dishes). Pour the oil into a glass bottle or jar and cork or seal. *Makes 1 cup.*

HERB-INFUSED OIL

1 cup best-quality olive oil
1/2 cup fresh herbs, loosely packed
(use "woody" herbs such as rosemary, thyme, sage, bay, oregano, etc.)
1 clove garlic, peeled

Set aside the best leaves or sprigs to display in the bottle. Put the rest of the herbs and garlic in a saucepan with the oil. Heat gently for 20 minutes. Do not allow herbs to brown. Let oil cool, then strain. Save garlic clove. Put flavored oil, garlic clove, and best leaves or sprigs in a glass bottle. Cork or seal. As you use the oil, remove herbs if they aren't completely immersed. (Herbs will become moldy in bottle if not completely covered with oil.) *Makes 1 cup.*

COMPOUND BUTTERS

Combine one stick (4 ounces) of unsalted butter, softened, with any of the following ingredients:

2 tablespoons freshly minced basil, 1 teaspoon lemon juice.

3 tablespoons finely chopped black olives, 2 tablespoons bleu cheese.

2 tablespoons crumbled bleu cheese, 1 teaspoon Worcestershire, 1 tablespoon minced onion, 1 tablespoon minced chives.

3 tablespoons crushed, drained capers; 1 teaspoon lemon zest, salt and pepper.

3 tablespoons minced fresh chives, 1 tablespoon parsley, salt and pepper to taste.

2 to 3 minced large garlic cloves, salt and pepper to taste.

2 teaspoons freshly grated lime zest, 1/4 teaspoon Tabasco.

1/2 cup nuts (pistachio, pecan, macadamia, etc.)

2 tablespoons freshly chopped tarragon, 1 tablespoon tarragon vinegar, a dash of Tabasco.

2 teaspoons soy sauce, 2 minced garlic cloves, 1 tablespoon peeled and minced fresh ginger.

Mix softened butter with your choice of ingredients. Place butter in middle of a sheet of foil or plastic wrap and roll into a cylinder. Wrap and chill until ready to slice and serve. Or freeze for later use.

Easy Grilling

QUE TIPS

GRILL GADGETS

The Que Queens like to have an assortment of grill toys. Our favorites are perforated black porcelain coated grill racks and grill baskets. The racks are great for grilling fish fillets, scallops, shrimp, and vegetables that might otherwise fall through larger grill grates. The basket is wok-shaped and allows for stir-grilling an assortment of sliced or julienne vegetables and other small food items without the fat of stir-frying.

HERB PAINT BRUSH

For basting, make an herb "paint" brush by selecting several long stalks of fresh rosemary, sage, tarragon, dill, etc. or a combination of several herbs and tie them together with twine. Dip brush into a baste of herb-infused oil or garlic butter and "paint" onto the vegetables or meats using a regal sweeping motion. A fragrant herbal flavor will be imparted to your fare, plus the aroma will be heavenly.

...MORE ON HERBS

Just for the fun of it, throw fresh herbs or water-soaked dry herbs on your grill fire. The aroma will linger and actually impart an herb flavor to your dining experience. Remember that flavor comes from all your senses and especially your sense of appreciation! Another great grill gadget is the hinged herb grill rack. Open the rack and place herbs on one side then close shut. Lay on top of the grill, place meat or vegetables on top of the rack and cook. Herbs please his and her majesty's!

KEBOB-BOB-ARAM

The Que Queens like the conviviality of having their guests participating in the grilling process. Our kebob equipment of choice is the kebob basket, a long narrow stainless steel basket that you just drop your meat and veggies into. No More Metal Skewers is a motto we've adapted from the famous movie queen Joan Crawford.

QUE TIPS

SKEWERS

We suggest double wooden skewers (they need to soak for 30 minutes prior to using on the grill). They are inexpensive and prohibit food from spinning, since they are doubled. This makes it easier to turn the skewered food during the cooking process. If you do use "metal" skewers, they need to be flat or double pronged and thread the chunks of food on loosely.

COLOR FOR THE PALATE

Beautiful shapes, sizes, and colors of tasty vegetables are available almost year-round. Kings, queens, and the rest of the court will be pleased when you offer fresh red and yellow sliced tomatoes overlapping on a pretty glass platter sprinkled with some fresh green basil or parsley, and garnished with some bright red cherry and miniature pear-shaped yellow tomatoes. Stir-grill a cascade of colored bell peppers together. Offer an assortment of russet, new, blue, and sweet potatoes that are slivered, seasoned, and grilled. Get the picture...in technicolor?!

PERFECT FISH AND SEAFOOD

Don't fool around like the court jester and over-cook fish and seafood. Fish will change from a translucent color to opaque. It's done when the flesh just begins to flake when tested with a fork. The royal rule is to cook fish 10 minutes per inch of thickness.

JAM AND JELLY

Jam, jellies and fruit preserves make for a quick delicious glaze for pork and poultry. (Apricot is particularly good.) Gently heat to melt and baste on pork or poultry using a pastry brush during the last 5 to 10 minutes of cooking.

A Razzle Dazzle Raspberry Feast

Raspberry Glazed Pork Tenderloin*

Raspberry Barbecue Chutney *

Herb Grilled Summer Squash*

Mario's Marvelous Pasta Salad*

**Mixed Baby Greens
with Vinaigrette Dressing**

Raspberry Almond Cheesecake*

Royal raspberries are a Que Queen favorite. This menu celebrates the joy of summer and stars the "queen" of the season's fruits. For an elegant touch, serve a Kir Royale (a glass of champagne with a little raspberry liqueur) or enjoy a frosty mug of micro-brewed wheat beer enlivened with the most regal of berries.

* RECIPE INCLUDED

RASPBERRY GLAZED PORK TENDERLOIN

2–3 pork tenderloins (about 2 pounds total)
1 cup raspberry barbecue sauce

Marinate the pork tenderloins in barbecue sauce for 1 hour. Grill over a hot fire for about 8 minutes on each side, basting with the sauce, until browned and meat thermometer registers 150 to 155 degrees. Serve with Raspberry Barbecue Chutney. *Serves 4.*

Fold and tie thin ends of tenderloins underneath for even thickness during cooking.

RASPBERRY BARBECUE CHUTNEY

1/2 cup raspberry barbecue sauce
2 tablespoons olive oil
3 tablespoons raspberry vinegar
1 teaspoon curry powder
1/2 cup chopped green onion
1 cup chopped apple
1 jalapeno pepper, chopped
1/2 cup raisins

Whisk the barbecue sauce, olive oil, raspberry vinegar, and curry powder in a medium bowl. Add the onion, apple, pepper, and raisins. Cover and keep refrigerated until ready to use. *Serves 4.*

For a change of taste, substitute raspberry preserves or frozen raspberries for the raspberry barbecue sauce.

HERB GRILLED SUMMER SQUASH

4 small summer squash (pattypan, zucchini, or crookneck)
4 tablespoons olive oil
1/2 cup chopped fresh herbs (parsley, chives, tarragon)
Salt and freshly ground black pepper to taste

Wash, pat dry and slice the squash about 1-inch thick on the diagonal. Put the squash and olive oil in a resealable plastic bag and coat well. Place squash in a greased grill basket and grill over a hot fire for 7 to 10 minutes, tossing every 2 to 3 minutes. The squash are done with they're soft, but not mushy. Toss the squash with fresh herbs, salt and pepper. *Serves 4.*

MARIO'S MARVELOUS PASTA SALAD

3/4 pound pasta (vermicelli, rotini and/or shell), cooked
2 tablespoons Romano cheese
3/4 cup bottled Italian dressing
1/2 cup mayonnaise (regular or light)
1 tablespoon Dijon mustard
1 teaspoon sugar
2 tablespoons chopped fresh parsley
2 teaspoons dried basil
1 teaspoon dried oregano
1 teaspoon salt
1/2 cup each of chopped: green pepper, red onion, tomato, carrot

Rinse cooked pasta in cold water and drain. In a separate bowl, mix the cheese, dressing, mayonnaise, mustard, sugar, herbs, and salt together. Combine pasta and vegetables in a large serving bowl, add dressing, and blend. Cover and chill until ready to serve. *Serves 4 to 6.*

This wonderful pasta salad is a most popular dish at Mario's of Westport (Kansas City, MO). The restaurant has had so many requests for the recipe, that printed copies of it are now kept on hand for inquiring customers. Our thanks to Mario's!

RASPBERRY ALMOND CHEESECAKE

1 pound cream cheese, softened
3 eggs
2/3 cup, plus 3 tablespoons sugar
1 teaspoon almond extract
8 ounces sour cream
1 teaspoon vanilla extract
1 cup fresh raspberries

Preheat oven to 350 degrees. Beat softened cream cheese with the eggs, 2/3 cup sugar, and almond extract until smooth, thick, and lemon colored. Pour the filling into a greased 9-inch pie pan. Bake for 25 minutes. Remove from oven and cool for 20 minutes. While cheesecake cools, mix sour cream, remaining 3 tablespoons sugar, and vanilla extract together. Pour over cooled cake, return to oven, and bake 10 minutes longer. Remove and let cool. Before serving, arrange raspberries on top of cheesecake.

This easy no-crust cheesecake can be made with the berries of any season. Try it with strawberries, blueberries or blackberries. They are all "berry" good.

A Funtastic Fiesta

Southwest Chicken Breasts*

Herb Grilled Chicken Breasts*

Jicama and Fruit Relish*

Garden Vegetable Stir Grill*

Mexicali Corn Pudding*

Luscious Lemon Pie*

The Que Queens love to celebrate...at the drop of a sombrero, any event can become reason for a festival. This fiesta menu, featuring popular flavors of the Southwest, will put everyone in a festive mood. Ole!!!

* RECIPE INCLUDED

SOUTHWEST CHICKEN BREASTS

2 whole chicken breasts, skinned, boned, and split (about 1 pound each)
2 tablespoons olive oil
4 cloves garlic, peeled
1/4 cup fresh mint leaves
1/4 cup freshly squeezed lime juice
1 teaspoon red pepper flakes

Place olive oil, garlic, mint, lime juice, and pepper flakes in a blender. Puree until thick. Place chicken breasts in glass dish and spoon puree over each piece. Let stand for 30 minutes, turning once. Grill chicken breasts over medium hot fire for 12 minutes, turning chicken once, until brown and firm to the touch. *Serves 4.*

HERB GRILLED CHICKEN BREASTS

2 whole chicken breasts, skinned, boned, and split (about 1 pound each)
Olive oil
Freshly ground pepper
Assortment of fresh herb sprigs (rosemary, thyme, tarragon, fennel)

Lightly oil and pepper chicken. Place herbs on an herb grill rack and set rack over a medium hot fire. Place chicken on herb rack and grill for 12 minutes, turning chicken once, until golden brown and firm to the touch. *Serves 4.*

Grilled chicken is a year-round favorite and so versatile! For different flavors, it's as simple as basting with soy, mustard, barbecue sauce–whatever suits your mood and menu. Grill chicken as directed above, basting the last 4 or 5 minutes. Grill extra chicken–to star in tomorrow's barbecue pizza or atop a Caesar salad.

JICAMA AND FRUIT RELISH

4 tablespoons freshly squeezed lime juice
4 tablespoons olive oil
1/2 teaspoon brown sugar
1/4 teaspoon sea salt
3 small seedless oranges
1 small mango
1 large tart apple
1 cup jicama, diced
1 tablespoon chili powder
1 teaspoon red pepper

Combine lime juice, olive oil, brown sugar, salt, and set aside. Peel oranges, mango and apple, and cut into bite-size chunks. Combine fruits and jicama in large glass bowl. Sprinkle with chili powder and red pepper. Immediately pour juice mixture over fruit, toss, and chill. *Serves 8.*

Relish keeps, refrigerated, for up to a week, although texture is best if served within two days.

GARDEN VEGETABLE STIR GRILL

1 pint cherry tomatoes, whole
2 small zucchini, sliced
2 small yellow squash, sliced
1 red onion, sliced
1 bell pepper, green/red/or yellow, sliced
1/2 cup Italian salad dressing

Rinse and prepare vegetables. Place in a large bowl, add salad dressing, and marinate for 1/2 hour. Pour mixture into a greased grill basket over the sink (to drain dressing). Grill for about 10 to 12 minutes over a hot fire, tossing several times, then serve at once. Vegetables will be crisp-tender. *Serves 8.*

MEXICALI CORN PUDDING

2 (11-ounce) cans Mexicorn
1/4 cup chopped green onion (white and green parts)
3 tablespoons all-purpose flour
2 teaspoons sugar
1/4 teaspoon salt
1/4 teaspoon ground red pepper
3 eggs, beaten
1 cup milk

Preheat oven to 350 degrees. Grease a 2-quart casserole and add the corn, onions, flour, sugar and seasonings. Stir to combine. In a small bowl, blend the eggs and milk together and pour over the corn. Bake casserole for 1 hour or until a knife inserted in the center comes out clean. *Serves 8.*

LUSCIOUS LEMON PIE

3 lemons
1 (14-ounce) can low fat sweetened condensed milk
1 prepared graham cracker pie crust
1/2 pint whipping cream or 1 (8-ounce) container whipped topping

Grate the lemon zest of 1 lemon into a mixing bowl. Add the juice of all three lemons. Blend in the condensed milk and pour into the pie crust. Refrigerate until firm. Whip the cream and serve each portion with a generous dollop. *Serves 8.*

Chop! Chop! Chop!

Lamb Chops with Chiles and Mint*

Ginger Lemon Pork Chops*

Sage Grilled Veal Chops*

**Watercress Salad with
Red Onion and Orange***

Sauteed Pea Pods

Assorted Crostini*

Cappuccino Pudding Cake*

When royal appetites can't agree—pork, veal, or lamb, what shall it be? The Queens say—all three! However, if your bunch is less unruly, any one of these chop recipes easily serves 4 people.

* RECIPE INCLUDED

LAMB CHOPS WITH CHILES AND MINT

8 lamb chops, 3/4-inch thick
2 small cloves garlic, peeled and minced
The juice of 1/2 lemon
2 small hot chile peppers, minced
1/2 cup chopped fresh mint

In a food processor, put the garlic, lemon juice, chiles, and mint; puree. Spread puree over lamb chops and marinate, refrigerated, for 30 minutes. Grill over hot fire until browned on the outside, but pink on the inside, about 4 minutes per side. *Serves 4.*

GINGER LEMON PORK CHOPS

4 (6 ounce) boneless pork chops, 1-inch thick
2 tablespoons lemon juice
2 tablespoons soy sauce
1 teaspoon grated fresh ginger

Combine lemon juice, soy sauce, and ginger. Pour over pork chops and marinate, refrigerated, for one hour. Grill over medium fire about 5 to 6 minutes per side. *Serves 4.*

SAGE GRILLED VEAL CHOPS

4 (6 to 8-ounce) veal chops, 3/4-inch thick
Olive oil
16 fresh sage leaves

Brush both sides of each chop with olive oil. Press 2 sage leaves on both sides of each chop and marinate, refrigerated, for one hour. Grill over hot fire about 5 to 6 minutes per side. *Serves 4.*

WATERCRESS SALAD WITH RED ONION AND ORANGE

1/3 cup light olive oil
1/3 cup fresh orange juice
The juice of 1 lime
Salt and freshly ground pepper
1 large bunch watercress, trimmed
2 oranges, peeled and white pith removed
1 medium red onion, thinly sliced

In a small bowl, mix together the olive oil, orange juice, lime juice, salt and pepper; set aside. Slice the oranges crosswise into thin rounds. Arrange the watercress on a large plate or platter. Top with orange and red onion slices. Pour vinaigrette over all. *Serves 4.*

ASSORTED CROSTINI

1 loaf firm textured bread, sliced about 1/2-inch thick
Olive oil
2 garlic cloves, peeled
Your choice of toppings

Brush olive oil and rub garlic over each side of sliced bread. Grill over a medium fire, about 2 to 3 minutes, until light brown. Top with your favorite ingredients. Suggestions: pesto, brie, chopped fresh tomato and shredded fresh basil, marinated peppers and feta cheese, marinated mushrooms and shaved Parmesan, mayonnaise blended with blue cheese and chopped black olives. *Serves 4 to 6.*

French and Italian bread work well for crostini. For additional tasty toppings, try the Greek Isle, Mediterranean, and Fiesta Burger Filling recipes on pages 43 and 44.

CAPPUCCINO PUDDING CAKE

1 cup all-purpose flour
2/3 cup sugar
2 tablespoons, plus 1/4 cup cocoa powder
2 teaspoons baking powder
1/4 teaspoon salt
1/2 cup evaporated milk
1 teaspoon vegetable oil
1 teaspoon vanilla extract
1/4 cup semisweet chocolate chips
1 cup firmly packed dark brown sugar
1-3/4 cups hot water
1/4 cup instant flavored coffee mix

Preheat oven to 350 degrees. Combine the flour, sugar, 2 tablespoons of the cocoa, baking powder, and salt in a 9-inch baking pan and stir to blend. Add milk, oil, and vanilla extract; stir again. Blend in chocolate chips. Combine brown sugar with the remaining 1/4 cup cocoa powder and sprinkle over the batter. Do not stir. Combine hot water with flavored coffee mix and pour over batter. Do not stir. Bake at 350 degrees for 40 minutes, or until cake springs back to the touch. Serve warm with a dollop of whipped cream or vanilla ice cream. *Serves 9.*

Try Suisse Mocha or Cafe Viennese for the instant coffee mix.

Here's an easy recipe for making your own flavored coffee mix: combine 1/2 cup instant espresso granules, 2/3 cup sugar, 2/3 cup powdered creamer, 1/2 teaspoon ground cinnamon. Store in a covered jar. To make a serving, add 2 teaspoons of mix to 1 cup of very hot water and stir well. Makes about 2 cups dry mix.

Lazy Days of Summer

Tarragon Grilled Turkey Breast*

Quick Apricot Chutney*

Summertime Corn and Cracked Wheat Salad*

Steamed Fresh Asparagus

**Grilled Focaccia with
Caramelized Onions and Brie***

**Grilled Fresh Pineapple
with Pineapple Sorbet***

A light and easy summertime feast. This marinated and grilled turkey comes out moist and delicious—fit for a queen. The turkey must be attended to during the entire grilling process. So the accompaniments selected here can all be prepared ahead of time. Invite your guests to arrive early, serve cold drinks, and enjoy entertaining while you baste the bird.

* RECIPE INCLUDED

TARRAGON GRILLED TURKEY BREAST

1 whole turkey breast, split
Salt and pepper to taste
1/2 cup white wine or tarragon vinegar
1/3 cup peanut oil
1/2 tablespoon poultry seasoning
1 teaspoon dried tarragon
1 teaspoon garlic powder
1 teaspoon hot sauce
1 teaspoon lemon juice

Rinse turkey breast and season well with salt and pepper. Combine remaining ingredients in a large resealable plastic bag. Add turkey breast, seal tightly, turn several times, refrigerate, and marinate for 1 hour. Remove turkey from bag, reserving marinade. Grill over medium hot fire for 45 to 60 minutes, turning and basting with reserved marinade every 5 minutes. Turkey is done when internal temperature reaches 170 to 175 degrees. *Serves 6 to 8.*

QUICK APRICOT CHUTNEY

1-1/2 cups apricot preserves
1/2 teaspoon grated fresh ginger
1/3 cup golden raisins
1/4 cup snipped dried apples
1 clove garlic, minced
2 tablespoons cider vinegar
1 teaspoon sea salt
1/4 teaspoon ground cinnamon
1/2 teaspoon white pepper

Combine all ingredients and mix well. Set aside for at least 1 hour before serving. Refrigerate unused portions in a tightly covered container. *Makes about 2 cups.*

SUMMERTIME CORN AND CRACKED WHEAT SALAD

1 cup cracked wheat or bulgur
2 cups warm water
1 (10-ounce) packaged frozen shoe peg corn, cooked and drained
2 tomatoes, finely chopped
4 green onions, finely chopped including some green
1 small cucumber, seeded and finely chopped
3 tablespoons chopped parsley
1/4 cup olive oil
1 tablespoon lemon juice
Salt and freshly ground pepper to taste

Combine cracked wheat and warm water in a small bowl for 1 hour. Drain off any remaining water and squeeze wheat dry. Combine wheat, corn, tomatoes, onions, cucumber, and parsley in a medium-sized bowl. Whisk oil and lemon juice together and pour over the salad. Toss to combine. *Serves 6 to 8.*

GRILLED FOCACCIA WITH CARAMELIZED ONIONS AND BRIE

2 fully baked 8-inch focaccia or pizza shells
2 tablespoons unsalted butter
2 large onions, peeled and thinly sliced
1/2 teaspoon sugar
2 tablespoons port
8 ounces Brie or Creme de Brie, cut into small pieces

In a large skillet over medium heat, melt butter and sauté onions. Sprinkle with sugar, drizzle with port, and continue to sauté until onions turn golden. Spread onions over each focaccia and dot with cubes of Brie. Grill over medium fire with the lid closed for 3 minutes or until the Brie melts. *Serves 6 to 8.*

This tasty-topped bread, cut into squares, is also very good as an appetizer. And do make extra caramelized onions. They are a marvelous addition to mashed potatoes or pasta. And try some on your favorite burger.

GRILLED FRESH PINEAPPLE

1 large fresh pineapple, peeled and cored

Right before serving, cut the pineapple into 1-inch thick rings and place in a grill basket. Grill over medium heat, about 2 minutes per side, until the pineapple has browned and softened. To serve, place a scoop of pineapple sorbet in each grilled pineapple ring. *Serves 6 to 8.*

PINEAPPLE SORBET

1 (20-ounce) can crushed pineapple in heavy syrup, frozen and unopened
3 tablespoons dark rum or 2 teaspoons rum flavoring
3 tablespoons canned cream of coconut

Submerge the unopened can of frozen pineapple in hot water for 1 minute. Open can and pour syrup into a food processor. Cut the frozen fruit into chunks and add to the processor. Puree until smooth; add rum and cream of coconut, stir. Serve immediately or freeze until ready to serve, up to 8 hours. *Makes 3 cups.*

Do not use light or water packed fruit in sorbet. Heavy syrup is integral to the process.

In the mood for mango? Try this variation of sorbet recipe: For ingredients listed, substitute 2 (15-ounce) cans mango slices in heavy syrup, frozen at least 18 hours and unopened, 1/4 cup Triple Sec, 2 tablespoons fresh lemon or lime juice. Proceed as directed. (If your food processor is small, make 1/2 recipe at a time and combine after pureeing.)

Dad-Doesn't-Cook-Today Picnic

Marinated Mushrooms*

Kansas City Strip Steak with
Parmesan Grilled Vegetables*

Absolutely Decadent Potatoes*

Two Greens and a Bean Salad*

Sliced Tomatoes Drizzled
with Flavored Olive Oil

Rhubarb Peach Crisp*

Ice Cream

Make this special dinner for a special guy—on Father's Day, or his birthday...or make any day special with this menu composed of all his favorites. A little indulgent? Yes, but the Queens believe their kings should be pampered!

* RECIPE INCLUDED

KANSAS CITY STRIP STEAKS
WITH PARMESAN GRILLED VEGETABLES

4 Kansas City strip steaks, 1-inch thick
2 cloves garlic, minced
4 teaspoons dried basil
2 teaspoons freshly ground black pepper
1/2 cup grated Parmesan cheese
1/4 cup olive oil
1/4 cup red wine vinegar
2 red or yellow bell peppers
2 large red onions

Combine garlic, basil, pepper and rub each steak with 2 teaspoons of mixture; set the rest of the mixture aside. In a small bowl, add the cheese, oil, vinegar and remaining seasoning mixture and set aside. Quarter and seed the peppers. Peel and cut the onion into 1/2-inch slices and precook in the microwave on high for 1-1/2 to 2 minutes. Place vegetables in a greased grill basket and place steaks directly on the grill. Cook both over a hot fire. Grill vegetables for about 15 minutes, tossing and brushing with the cheese mixture the last 10 minutes of cooking. Grill the steaks for 7 minutes on each side for medium. *Serves 4.*

MARINATED MUSHROOMS

1 pound fresh small button mushrooms, cleaned
1/2 cup vinegar
1/4 cup olive oil
1 clove garlic, minced

Combine mushrooms with other ingredients in a glass bowl. Marinate, refrigerated, overnight or for several hours. *Serves 4.*

For a change of taste, try experimenting with your favorite flavored vinegars and oils.

ABSOLUTELY DECADENT POTATOES

1 (24-ounce) package frozen hash brown potatoes
1 teaspoon garlic powder
Salt and pepper to taste
1/4 cup melted butter
3/4 cup heavy cream
2 tablespoons chopped chives (optional)

Thaw hash browns enough to flake with a fork. In a greased 2 quart casserole, layer a third each of the potatoes, seasonings, and butter. Repeat. Recipe can be prepared to this point, then covered and refrigerated. (Prepare no sooner than morning of day you plan to serve.) Preheat oven to 300 degrees. Pour cream over potatoes and bake for 2 hours or until potatoes are browned and bubbling. Remove from oven and stir well before serving. Sprinkle chives over top if desired. *Serves 4.*

Joan Johnson of Amherst, Wisconsin, serves these wonderful and easy potatoes at family gatherings all year round...because they've become such a favorite. And they're such a favorite with the Que Queens, we've voted to make Joan an Honorary Que Queen!

TWO GREENS AND A BEAN SALAD

6 ounces spiral-shaped pasta
4 cups coarsely chopped spinach leaves
4 cups coarsely chopped escarole leaves
2 tablespoons olive oil
Salt and pepper to taste
1 (19-ounce) can cannellini beans or other white beans, drained
2 cloves garlic, minced
1/2 cup shredded Asiago or Parmesan cheese

Cook the pasta according to package directions; drain well. Combine warm pasta with the other ingredients and toss well. Serve immediately. *Serves 4.*

RHUBARB PEACH CRISP

6 to 8 large, ripe peaches, peeled and sliced
Juice of 1 lemon
1-1/2 to 2 cups sugar
1 tablespoon flour
4 to 6 stalks rhubarb, chopped
1/2 cup water
1/2 cup (1 stick) butter
1 cup each: flour, brown sugar, and oatmeal
1/2 cup molasses
1/2 teaspoon cinnamon

In a large (9 x 13-inch) casserole, arrange the peaches and drizzle with lemon juice so they keep their color. Take 1 tablespoon of sugar and 1 tablespoon of flour and dust over the peaches and toss to coat. Set aside. Put the rhubarb in a saucepan with the water and 1 to 1-1/2 cups sugar. Simmer until the rhubarb is soft. Add more sugar if necessary. Pour the rhubarb over the peaches and toss together. Set aside.

In a large skillet, melt the butter and add the flour, brown sugar, oatmeal, molasses and cinnamon. Simmer together for 5 minutes until the mixture is hot and bubbling. Let cool for about 5 minutes until the mixture is cool enough not to burn your fingers, but warm enough to be pliable. Pat the mixture gently over the fruit. Bake at 350 degrees for 50 minutes. *Serves 8.*

Our thanks to Que Queen Lou Jane Temple for this unique recipe. It's a Royal Favorite. Lou Jane's culinary mystery novel, "Revenge of the Barbeque Queens," is also a favorite of ours. It has us wondering, though, just which character is based on which real-life Queen ... ???

Hook, Line, and Sizzle

**Salmon Steaks with
Grilled Red Onion Slices***

Balsamic Mustard Grilled Swordfish*

Cherry Tomatoes with Snipped Chives*

Grilled Asparagus*

Parsleyed New Potatoes in Foil*

**Old-Fashioned Lemon Verbena Pound Cake
with Lemonade Glaze***

Reel them in with this grilled seafood dinner. (The cook decides whether to prepare salmon or swordfish.) While the fragrant and lovely cake is baked ahead of time, the rest of the meal assembles in minutes.

* RECIPE INCLUDED

SALMON STEAKS WITH GRILLED RED ONION SLICES

4 (6-ounce) salmon steaks or fillets
1 red onion, peeled and sliced thickly
1/4 cup teriyaki sauce
2 tablespoons vinegar
4 cloves garlic, minced
1 teaspoon dried ginger
1 teaspoon sesame oil

Rinse fish thoroughly and place in a glass dish, topped with onion slices. Combine the teriyaki sauce, vinegar, garlic, ginger, and oil. Pour over salmon and onion slices. Marinate for 15 to 30 minutes. Remove salmon and onion from the marinade and place on a greased grill rack. Grill over hot fire for 10 minutes per inch of thickness of the fish. *Serves 4.*

BALSAMIC MUSTARD GRILLED SWORDFISH

4 large swordfish steaks
3 tablespoons balsamic vinegar
4 tablespoons olive oil
1/2 cup Dijon mustard

Rinse fish thoroughly and place in a glass dish. Combine the vinegar, oil, and mustard, and pour over fish. Marinate, refrigerated, for 15 to 30 minutes. Drain the fish and reserve the marinade. Grill the swordfish over a hot fire for 5 to 6 minutes per side (10 minutes per inch of thickness), basting with the marinade several times while cooking. The fish is done when it just begins to flake apart. *Serves 4.*

Marinate fish for about 30 minutes only, as it tends to get mushy if over-marinated.

CHERRY TOMATOES WITH SNIPPED CHIVES

1 pint cherry tomatoes
2 tablespoons olive oil or salad dressing
1/2 cup Feta cheese, crumbled
1 tablespoon snipped chives

Rinse and halve tomatoes. Put in shallow bowl, pour oil over tomatoes, toss to mix; top with cheese and garnish with snipped chives. *Serves 4.*

GRILLED ASPARAGUS

1 pound fresh asparagus, trimmed
Marinade of your choice

Make up extra of either fish marinade shown on previous page to use on the asparagus. Lay asparagus spears out flat on a baking tray. Brush half the marinade over asparagus. Grease a grill basket or rack and grill asparagus until crisp-tender and slightly charred. Drizzle remaining marinade over hot asparagus. *Serves 4.*

PARSLEYED NEW POTATOES IN FOIL

1-1/2 pounds new potatoes, cleaned
2 tablespoons butter
1/4 cup finely chopped parsley
Salt and pepper to taste

In a saucepan, cover the potatoes with water and boil for about 10 minutes, or until almost done; drain and set aside. Tear off a large sheet of aluminum foil. Put the potatoes on foil, dot with butter, sprinkle with parsley, salt and pepper. Close up foil package and grill for 10 minutes, turning once. *Serves 4.*

OLD FASHIONED LEMON VERBENA POUND CAKE
WITH LEMONADE GLAZE

1 cup butter, softened
3 cups sugar
1/4 teaspoon salt
6 eggs, at room temperature
3 cups all-purpose flour
1 cup sour cream
2 teaspoons grated lemon zest
1 teaspoon vanilla extract
12 to 15 fresh lemon verbena or lemon geranium leaves, washed and dried
1/2 cup lemon juice
1 cup sugar

Preheat the oven to 350 degrees. Butter and flour a 10-inch bundt or tube pan. In a large bowl, cream together butter, sugar, and salt using an electric mixer. Add eggs, one by one, beating well after each addition.Stir in the flour, then add sour cream. Add lemon zest and vanilla extract. Place the lemon verbena leaves in a pattern around bottom of pan. Pour batter in carefully. Bake 1-1/4 hours or until a wooden toothpick inserted in the middle comes out clean. Transfer to a rack to cool for 10 minutes. Meanwhile, put the lemon juice and sugar in a saucepan and bring to a boil; cook for 5 minutes and set aside. Invert the cake onto a rack. Brush glaze over the warm cake and let cool. *Serves 10 to 12.*

The lemon verbena leaves make a lovely pattern on this delicious cake. You can also use lemon or rose geranium leaves.

For a festive but simple alternative dessert, try this Merry Sherry Cake recipe from an Honorary Que Queen, Mary Ann Duckers: combine 1 yellow cake mix (with pudding in mix), 1 box instant vanilla pudding mix, 1 teaspoon nutmeg, 4 eggs, 1 cup cream sherry and 3/4 cup cooking oil in a large bowl. Beat for 5 minutes and pour in greased bundt pan. Bake at 350 degrees for 45 to 50 minutes. Cool in pan on a rack for 10 minutes. Then invert onto rack and let cool completely. Sprinkle with powdered sugar before serving.

Kebob-a-Rama

Greek Kofta Kebobs*

Beef & Veggie Bobs*

Chicken Tikka Kebobs*

Onion, Cucumber, and Tomato Raita*

Garden Vegetable Couscous*

**Baby Greens with Goat Cheese,
Sunflower Seeds, and Balsamic Vinaigrette**

Warm Pita Bread

Easy-Breezy Blackberry Picnic Torte*

"Lavish" is a favorite word in any Queen's vocabulary, and this delightful meal proves that lavish doesn't have to be difficult. Kebobs are a fun way to entertain. Arrange the ingredients and skewers on a table near the grill and let guests put together their favorite kebobs—and grill them too.

* RECIPE INCLUDED

GREEK KOFTA KEBOBS

3/4 pound ground lamb
2/3 cup Italian seasoned bread crumbs
1/2 cup grated onion
2 cloves garlic, minced
1-1/2 tablespoons chopped fresh parsley
1/2 teaspoon ground cinnamon
1/4 teaspoon ground ginger
1 egg, beaten
Salt and pepper to taste

Combine all ingredients and blend well. Dampen hands and form mixture into 16 meatballs. Chill until firm, several hours or overnight. Place meatballs in kebob baskets. Grill over a hot fire, turning baskets several times to brown the meatballs evenly. Grill 12 to 15 minutes or until meatballs are brown and crisp. *Serves 4.*

BEEF AND VEGGIE BOBS

1 pound beef sirloin steak, cut into 1-inch cubes
1 zucchini, cut into 1-inch slices
1 small eggplant, cut into 1-inch cubes
2 ears fresh sweet corn, cut into 8 pieces
1 large red onion, cut into 8 wedges
1/2 cup Italian salad dressing

Combine all ingredients in a large resealable plastic bag. Marinate in the refrigerator for at least an hour or overnight. Place ingredients in 4 kebob baskets. Grill over a hot fire for 8 to 10 minutes, turning once, until corn is tender and beef is medium rare to medium. *Serves 4.*

CHICKEN TIKKA KEBOBS

1-1/2 pounds chicken breasts, skinned and boned, cut into 1-inch pieces
2 tablespoons fresh lemon juice
1/2 teaspoon salt
1/4 cup plain yogurt (do not use fat free)
4 cloves garlic, minced
1-1/2 tablespoons ground coriander
3 teaspoons ground cumin
1 teaspoon ground turmeric
1 zucchini, cut into 1-inch slices
1 yellow squash, cut into 1-inch slices

Combine the chicken, lemon juice and salt in a medium bowl and let stand 30 minutes. Blend the yogurt, garlic, coriander, cumin, and turmeric; add to chicken and coat well. Cover and marinate at least 3 hours or overnight. When ready to cook, combine zucchini and yellow squash with chicken in kebob baskets. Grill kebobs over a hot fire, turning once, for 12 to 15 minutes. *Serves 4.*

Kebob baskets make grilling so easy! If you do use wooden skewers, soak them for at least 30 minutes before assembling.

ONION, CUCUMBER, AND TOMATO RAITA

1/2 cup chopped onion
1/2 cup chopped, seeded cucumber
1 tomato, peeled, seeded and chopped
2 tablespoons fresh cilantro, chopped
2 fresh jalapeno peppers, chopped
1 cup plain yogurt (do not use fat free)

Combine all ingredients and serve. *Makes about 2 cups.*

GARDEN VEGETABLE COUSCOUS

2 cups chicken stock
1-1/2 cup couscous
2 chopped green onions
1 yellow bell pepper, seeded and chopped
1 cucumber, seeded and chopped
1 tomato, stemmed and chopped
2 tablespoons fresh snipped chives
2 tablespoons fresh lemon juice
Salt and pepper to taste

Bring chicken stock to a boil and pour over couscous in a large bowl. Let stand to absorb liquid, about 5 minutes, then fluff with a fork. Add remaining ingredients and serve. *Serves 4.*

EASY-BREEZY BLACKBERRY PICNIC TORTE

1 store-bought pound cake
1-1/2 cups blackberry jam
1 cup lemon yogurt

Slice pound cake lengthwise into 4 layers. Place bottom layer on a serving plate. Spread 1/3 of jam on the bottom layer. Top with the second layer of cake. Spread with jam. Repeat process once more. Refrigerate to set. Top with a dollop of chilled lemon yogurt just before serving. *Serves 8.*

Another quick treat, especially for chocolate lovers, is this Black Forest version: use chocolate pound cake and substitute cherry preserves for blackberry jam. Follow steps set out above. Top with sweetened whipped cream and sprinkle with chocolate shavings.

Fourth of July Burger Bonanza

Crudités with Garlic Dill Dipping Sauce

Burgers, Burgers, Burgers!*
Greek* Mediterranean* Fiesta* Veggie*

Platters of fresh sliced tomatoes,
lettuce, onions, cheeses

Hard rolls, hamburger buns,
rye bread, focaccia, pita, etc.

Grilled-in-the-Husk Corn on the Cob

French Herbed Potato Salad*

Spirited Watermelon*

Stars and Stripes Dessert Pizza*

The Queens celebrate Independence Day by taking over the grill and inviting each guest to bring a dish. You might want to do the same—be sure to furnish your guests with these special recipes. Then you can concentrate on a celebration of burgers.

* RECIPE INCLUDED

BURGERS FOR FOUR

1-1/2 pounds ground meat (choose from ground chuck, turkey, lamb or pork)
Garlic salt and freshly ground pepper

To prepare filled burgers: Divide each 1-1/2 pound portion of meat into 8 equal parts. Flatten each portion into 8 patties. Place a fourth of one of the following fillings in the center of 4 of the patties to within 1/2" of the perimeter. Gently place a second patty on top of filled one, pressing edges together. Sprinkle garlic salt and pepper on each burger. Grill over hot fire for 5 to 7 minutes per side. *Serves 4.*

When making any kind of filled burgers, form all the patties and make filling(s) the night before, but don't put the two together until right before you're ready to grill.

GREEK ISLE BURGER FILLING

1 large ripe tomato, finely chopped
2 tablespoons finely chopped red onion
4 ounces feta cheese, crumbled
2 tablespoons chopped black olives
1 teaspoon red wine vinegar
1 teaspoon olive oil
1/2 teaspoon dried oregano

Combine all ingredients in a small bowl and let marinate for at least 30 minutes before using. Wonderful on lamb or beef burgers. *Makes about 2 cups.*

MEDITERRANEAN BURGER FILLING

1/4 cup each: mayonnaise, grated Parmesan, chopped green onion and black olives

Combine all ingredients. Good with turkey and beef burgers. *Makes 1 cup.*

FIESTA BURGER FILLING

1/4 cup each: chopped tomato, jalapeno pepper, fresh cilantro, green onion

Combine all ingredients. Goes especially well with pork but is good with all burgers. *Makes 1 cup.*

These fillings also make wonderful toppings for Crostini. (See page 24.)

GRILLED TOMATO "BURGER"
WITH HERBED CREAM CHEESE

2 medium very firm ripe tomatoes
1 (8-ounce) package cream cheese, softened
1 clove garlic, minced
2 tablespoons fresh chopped basil
1 tablespoon fresh snipped chives
4 Kaiser rolls

Combine cream cheese, garlic, and herbs. Slice the Kaiser rolls and grill until warm. Spread the inside of each roll with the herbed cream cheese mixture. Slice each tomato into 4 thick slices, discarding the ends. Grill in a grill basket over a medium to hot fire for about 3 to 4 minutes per side. Place two slices on each bun and serve. *Serves 4.*

GRILLED PORTOBELLO MUSHROOM "BURGER"

4 large portobello mushrooms
2 tablespoons olive oil
1 garlic clove, peeled and minced
French bread or sesame seed hamburger buns

Blend the olive oil and garlic together. Brush on mushrooms. Grill over hot coals about 4 minutes per side. Place mushrooms on bread and serve. Add mayonnaise, lettuce and tomato, if desired. *Serves 4.*

FRENCH HERBED POTATO SALAD

6 large russet potatoes
3 tablespoons tarragon vinegar
1 bunch green onion, finely chopped
1/4 cup chopped fresh parsley
1/4 cup vegetable oil
1 clove garlic, minced
Salt and pepper to taste

Boil the unpeeled potatoes in salted water for 20 minutes or until done. Remove from water, cool, peel, and cut potatoes into 1/4-inch slices. Arrange slices in a large shallow bowl and sprinkle with the vinegar. Top with onion and parsley. Mix vegetable oil and garlic, then drizzle over potatoes. Sprinkle with salt and pepper to taste. Cover and let stand at room temperature until ready to serve. *Serves 8.*

SPIRITED WATERMELON

1 watermelon
1 to 2 cups rum or vodka

Cut a 2-inch deep hole plug into the top of the melon. Slowly pour liquor into melon until it can absorb no more. Replace the plug and seal with heavy tape.Chill for 6 to 8 hours or overnight. Slice and serve. *Serves 8.*

STARS AND STRIPES DESSERT PIZZA

3/4 package of refrigerated sugar cookie dough
1 (8-ounce) package cream cheese, softened
1/2 cup sugar
2 tablespoons lemon juice
1/2 cup cranberry juice
1/4 cup strawberry jelly
2 cups strawberries, sliced vertically
1 cup blueberries
13 miniature marshmallows

Pat cookie dough in the bottom of a 9 x 13-inch cookie sheet or jelly roll pan. Bake at 350 degrees for 8 to 10 minutes or until the cookie crust has browned. Remove from oven and set aside to cool. In a small bowl, combine the cream cheese, sugar, and lemon juice. Spread over the cooled cookie crust. In a small saucepan, heat cranberry juice and strawberry jelly until bubbly. Set aside to cool. Arrange the blueberries and miniature marshmallows in the upper left hand corner of the cookie crust to form the "stars." Arrange rows of strawberries to make the "stripes." With a small brush, glaze the strawberries and blueberries with the strawberry jelly mixture. Cover and refrigerate until ready to serve. *Serves 12 to 15.*

Simple Smoking

QUE TIPS

CITRUS SPRAY

The tang of fresh citrus is a luscious treat on grilled or smoked meats. Fill a spray bottle with apple cider, fruit juices, or combinations like apple, cranberry, orange, lemon, or lime to apply to ribs, pork, or chicken during the last fifteen minutes of cooking. The juice adds an attractive glaze and the faint sweet flavor will complement the meat.

ADOPT A MENTOR

If you have a friend or neighbor who draws rave reviews for his or her barbecue, volunteer to help them so you can learn their techniques. This is somewhat like being a page of the court...try it!

DEAR DIARY!

As you become more proficient with the basics, experiment to develop your own style. Keep a diary or barbecue journal on hand to record ingredients and measurements, cooking and basting times, fire temperature, kinds of woods used and such.

GADGETS FOR THE SMOKER

A marinade injector is a long needle nose syringe used to inject large tough cuts of meat with moisture. Rib racks are convenient for holding ribs upright, rather than by stacking them on top of each other. Thus, it's easy to rotate the ribs. Turning them around is a breeze with your long-handled, spring-loaded tongs...just like holding a scepter!

THE KING WAS IN THE COUNTING HOUSE

Watch for grocery store specials on large cuts of meat like brisket, whole turkey, roasts, and such to take advantage of best values. Smoked meats provide ample leftovers that can be turned into show-stoppers. Try tossing smoked salmon with pasta, butter, garlic, and cream sprinkled with Romano cheese. Leftover meats can be used as toppings for pizza, to stuff in tacos or fajitas, or turn a green salad into a main course. Plus, don't forget the Earl of Sandwich!

QUE TIPS

THE QUEEN WAS IN THE CUPBOARD

A well-stocked pantry makes meal planning a snap. Assorted canned beans make wonderful cold salads when rinsed, drained, and tossed with vinaigrette. Packaged dry goods like pasta, rice, couscous, and tabbouleh are great for quick side dishes. Staples like potatoes, onions, and winter squash cook nicely on the grill or in the smoker, too.

THE CROWNING GLORY OF FLAVOR

Marinades can impart wonderful flavor to the meats that you plan to grill or smoke. Always marinate in non-reactive containers; a glass dish will do. But the Que Queens' highly recommend plastic zip-lock bags. The bags allow for a more thorough over-all coating of the meat, plus you use less marinade. Clean-up is fast because you throw the bag away.

...MORE ON MARINADES OR *NO NO NANETTE*!

No, no, never ever reuse marinades to marinate anything else. Never! If you want to make up a batch of marinade ahead of time, do so by combining the oils and vinegars, but add fresh or dry herbs and seasonings (like basil, garlic, or freshly ground pepper) the day you plan to use the marinade for optimum strength.

NEATNIK ACCESSORIES

Along with our tiaras, the Que Queens like utilitarian accessories. Heavy-duty aluminum foil that can be crimped to make a disposable bowl. Aluminum pans are great for holding meats and their juices for basting. Grocery stores usually have a selection of all sizes and shapes of aluminum pans. Use them for side dishes in the smoker so you don't have the clean up.

SIMPLE SMOKING

This last Que Tip may cause charcoal purists to shout Off With Their Heads! For simple smoking, an electric water smoker is hard to beat. Just add the wood, fill the water pan, season the meat, place on the grill, and plug in the smoker. Use a meat thermometer or the manufacturer's time chart to know when your delicious food is ready!

A Royal Rib Feast

Que Queens Prize-Winning Barbecued Ribs*

Tuxedo Baked Beans*

Smoked Vegetables with Lemon-Rosemary Vinaigrette*

Tangy Coleslaw*

Fresh Blueberry Tart*

These are the ribs that beat the men's barbecue team and established us as barbecue royalty. So when we want to pull out all the stops and declare a feast day, this is what we serve. Although traditional accompaniments to barbecued ribs include baked or barbecued beans, coleslaw, hush puppies and fruit cobbler, we've streamlined this meal to fit our new regal status. Your guests will be pleased with this "royal treatment," especially when they try the fresh blueberry tart.

* RECIPE INCLUDED

QUE QUEENS PRIZE-WINNING BARBECUED RIBS

3 whole slabs of loin baby back pork ribs (about 4 pounds)

Rub:
4 tablespoons sugar
2 tablespoons garlic salt
2 tablespoons ground black pepper
2 tablespoons paprika
2 tablespoons celery salt

1(12-ounce) can of beer
1 (14-ounce) bottle of spicy tomato barbecue sauce

The day before cooking, use needle nose pliers to grab the membrane on the underside of each slab of ribs, and pull off in one motion. Prepare rub by combining dry ingredients; rub onto entire surface of the meat. Cover and let the flavors blend overnight in the refrigerator.

In a smoker build an indirect charcoal fire with a water pan on the other side. When the fire is hot, add about 3 chunks of water-soaked hickory and/or apple wood. Maintain a 225 degree temperature. Place the ribs in the cooker on a rack above the water pan (indirect heat) and smoke for about 2 hours, or until the meat pulls back from the bone about 1/2 inch. Turn the ribs over, baste with the beer, and cook for 1 hour more, basting every 10 to 15 minutes. The more moisture, the better the ribs. Finally, during the last 30 minutes of cooking, baste the ribs with spicy barbecue sauce. *Serves 6.*

To prepare your own flavored barbecue sauce add any of the following to one (14-ounce) bottle of tomato-based sauce:

2 tablespoons of your favorite rub mixture - for Spicy
2 teaspoons Liquid Smoke - for Smoky
1 cup raspberry preserves - for Raspberry
1/2 cup honey - for Sweet
2 tablespoons soy sauce and 2 teaspoons sesame oil - for Asian

TUXEDO BAKED BEANS

3 tablespoons vegetable oil
1 large red onion, diced
1 mild green chile, seeded and chopped finely
3 large garlic cloves, minced
1 cup sour cream
3 cups cooked black beans
2 cups corn, fresh, frozen, or canned white shoepeg (drained)
1/2 bunch fresh cilantro, chopped
Salt and freshly ground pepper to taste
1 cup grated sharp Cheddar cheese

Preheat oven to 375 degrees. Heat oil in a large skillet and sauté onion until transparent, about 5 minutes. Add the chile and garlic and sauté for 2 minutes more. Remove from heat and fold in sour cream. Add black beans, corn, cilantro, salt and pepper; pour mixture into an oiled baking dish. Sprinkle top with grated Cheddar and bake for 20 minutes, or until the casserole is bubbly and cheese has melted. *Serves 6*

SMOKED VEGETABLES WITH LEMON-ROSEMARY VINAIGRETTE

1/4 cup chopped fresh rosemary leaves (2 tablespoons dry)
1/2 cup olive oil
1/4 cup fresh lemon juice
Salt and pepper to taste
4 Vidalia, or other sweet onions, peeled and cut in sixths
6 tomatoes
2 yellow bell peppers, cored, seeded and cut in sixths
2 red bell peppers, cored, seeded and cut in sixths

Combine the rosemary, olive oil, lemon juice and seasonings in a large resealable plastic bag. Using a fork, scratch the surface of each vegetable. Place vegetables in bag with oil mixture, coat well and marinate for at least 30 minutes. Drain vegetables, reserving marinade, and lay them in a metal baking dish. Smoke at 225 degrees for 30 minutes to an hour, basting frequently, until the vegetables are soft. *Serves 6.*

TANGY COLESLAW

4 cups shredded Napa cabbage
1 cup shredded carrot
1 cup bottled vinaigrette salad dressing
1 teaspoon celery seed
Sugar to taste

Put shredded cabbage and carrot in a large bowl. Combine salad dressing, celery seed, and sugar. Pour over slaw and toss. *Serves 6.*

FRESH BLUEBERRY TART

1-1/2 cups all-purpose flour
1/2 cup melted butter
1-1/4 cups sugar
1 (8-ounce) package cream cheese, softened
1 egg, beaten
1 teaspoon vanilla
5 cups blueberries, rinsed
1/3 cup water

Preheat oven to 350 degrees. Combine flour, butter and 1/2 cup sugar. Pat mixture into the bottom and sides of an 8-inch springform pan. Bake for 12 minutes until lightly browned. Set aside to cool. Cream together the cream cheese, 1/4 cup sugar, egg and vanilla. Pour into the crust. Bake at 400 degrees for 20 to 25 minutes. Remove from oven and cool. Combine 3 cups of the blueberries with 1/3 cup water and 1/2 cup sugar in a heavy saucepan. Bring to a boil stirring constantly. Lower heat to a simmer and continue stirring until mixture thickens, about 15 minutes. Add remaining 2 cups of berries. Spread over the cream cheese tart filling and serve. *Serves 8.*

The blueberry sauce is excellent served over pound cake or angel food cake and topped with vanilla ice cream. Recipe can also be prepared with strawberries.

A Down-Home Dinner

Kansas City-Style Smoked Brisket*

Smoked Stuffed Mushrooms*

Horseradish Potatoes*

Marinated Green Bean Salad*

Espresso-Mocha Brownies*

Here's the next generation of down-home dinners—all the old favorites with a new twist. Nibble on the mushrooms while the brisket slowly smokes. Then end the meal with a rich chocolate dessert paired with the mellow flavor of coffee. Delicious!

* RECIPE INCLUDED

KANSAS CITY-STYLE SMOKED BRISKET

1 (10 to 12-pound) beef brisket, trimmed
1/2 cup paprika
1/4 cup cayenne pepper
1/4 cup granulated garlic
1/4 cup black pepper
Olive oil

Combine dry ingredients and set aside. Coat brisket with the olive oil and combine spices and rub into meat. Let sit for an hour to come to room temperature. In a smoker, prepare an indirect charcoal fire. Set a pan of water on the other side. When the fire is hot, add water-soaked chunks of hickory wood to the charcoal. When the heat registers 225 degrees, place the brisket over the water pan, cover, and monitor the temperature, keeping close to 225 degrees. Smoke the brisket for 12 hours, keeping temperature steady. Remove the brisket from smoker, wrap in plastic wrap, then cover completely with aluminum foil. Return the covered brisket to smoker and cook for another 3 hours. Remove from smoker and let stand for 10 minutes. Unwrap, then slice thinly and serve with your favorite barbecue sauce. *Serves 8 to 10.*

SMOKED STUFFED MUSHROOMS

24 large mushrooms, cleaned
2 tablespoons vegetable oil
1 medium onion, peeled and chopped
8 ounces cream cheese, softened
1/2 cup mozzarella cheese, shredded
2 teaspoons Italian seasoning
Salt and pepper to taste
2 tablespoons chopped fresh parsley

Stem mushrooms and chop stems finely. Heat the oil in a skillet and sauté stems and onion for about 5 minutes; set aside. In a food processor, blend the cream cheese, mozzarella, Italian seasoning, salt and pepper. Transfer to a bowl and blend in the parsley and onion mixture. Stuff the mushrooms. Put mushrooms in a greased grill basket or on a baking sheet and smoke over indirect heat for 1 hour. *Serves 8 to 10.*

HORSERADISH POTATOES

8 large potatoes, peeled and quartered
1 cup heavy cream
4 tablespoons butter
1 tablespoon horseradish, or to taste
Salt and pepper to taste

Put potatoes in a large pot and cover with water. Bring to a boil and cook for 15 minutes, or until the potatoes are done. Drain the water and mash with the cream and butter until smooth. Blend in the horseradish and season to taste. *Serves 8.*

For a change of taste, replace horseradish with 1/2 cup hot caramelized onions (see page 28 for recipe) or with 2 or 3 smoked, mashed cloves of garlic. To smoke garlic, cut 1/2 inch off the pointed end head of garlic. Drizzle with oil, then slow smoke until tender.

MARINATED GREEN BEAN SALAD

2 pounds fresh green beans, cleaned and stringed
1 red onion, slivered
4 tablespoons fresh chopped parsley
1/2 cup olive oil
1/3 cup white wine vinegar
4 teaspoons Dijon mustard
Salt and freshly ground pepper to taste

Bring a pot of salted water to a boil and add beans. Cook for 6 minutes or until crisp tender. Drain and immerse immediately in cold water. In a large bowl, combine the rest of the ingredients and stir to blend. Drain the green beans, add to the bowl, and toss with dressing. *Serves 8 to 10.*

ESPRESSO-MOCHA BROWNIES

6 ounces bitter chocolate
1 cup (2 sticks) margarine or butter
4 ounces espresso
2 cups sugar
2 teaspoons vanilla extract
4 eggs
1-1/2 cups chocolate chips (optional)
2 cups cake flour
1/2 teaspoon salt
2 teaspoons baking powder
Chopped walnuts (optional)

Preheat oven to 350 degrees. Together microwave chocolate and margarine for 2 minutes at a time, stirring until chocolate melts and mixture is smooth. Stir in espresso and cool to room temperature. In a large mixing bowl, combine sugar, vanilla, and eggs. Mix very well. Stir in chocolate mixture and add chocolate chips. Sift together flour, salt, and baking powder. Add to batter using a rubber spatula, stirring well (do not beat). Pour batter into a greased 9-by-13-inch baking pan. If using chopped walnuts, press them gently into batter. Bake for 30 to 40 minutes. When done, a toothpick will come out chocolate-coated, but not gooey with raw batter. *Serves 12.*

Turn this recipe into an elegant "torte" by baking in an 8-inch springform pan and frosting. An easy chocolate frosting: together microwave 1 cup half-and-half and 1-1/2 cups chocolate chips, stirring until chocolate melts. Cool and frost cake. This is an excellent hot fudge sauce, too.

Baa-Baa-Barbecue

Smoked Stuffed Leg of Lamb*

Smoky Tapenade*

Fettuccine with Smoked Garlic and Tomato*

Steamed Baby Vegetables

Fresh Fruit Ambrosia with Mint*

Lemon Balm Icebox Cookies*

This menu is perfect when the weather turns cooler, whether you're dining on a wine country terrace or in a wheat country back yard. Smoking heightens the flavors of these simple, yet sophisticated dishes. They are some of our favorites! A crisp rosé or cabernet sauvignon—or a cold, frosty mug of beer—makes it all taste better.

* RECIPE INCLUDED

SMOKED STUFFED LEG OF LAMB

1 (6 to 7-pound) leg of lamb, boned, trimmed and butterflied
1 pound spinach leaves, rinsed and stemmed
3 tablespoons olive oil
2 large cloves garlic, minced
1/2 cup fresh bread crumbs
1/4 cup raisins
1/4 cup pine nuts
1/4 cup fresh chopped basil
1 (3-ounce) package cream cheese
1/2 teaspoon salt
1/4 teaspoon ground pepper

Pat the spinach dry on paper towels. Take 10 to 12 large leaves and stack them on top of each other. Roll the leaves into a cigar shape and cut crosswise into 1/8-inch shreds. Repeat with the remaining spinach. In a medium skillet, heat the olive oil over high heat. Stir in the spinach and garlic, tossing and stirring often. Cook for 2 minutes or until the moisture has evaporated. Spoon the spinach mixture into a medium bowl and stir in the bread crumbs, raisins, pine nuts, basil, cream cheese, salt, and pepper. Lay out the butterflied lamb and spread with the spinach mixture. Roll up lengthwise, jelly roll style and tie with twine at 1-inch intervals. Smoke at 225 degrees over an indirect fire of hickory and apple wood for 5 to 6 hours or until a meat thermometer inserted into the thickest part registers at least 160 degrees for medium. *Serves 6 to 8.*

This outstanding recipe was developed by Que Queen Karen Putman.

SMOKY TAPENADE

3/4 cup wheat berries (available at health food stores)
2-1/4 cups water
1 cup pitted Kalamata or California black olives
1 clove garlic
1 teaspoon Dijon mustard
1/4 cup extra-virgin olive oil
Country-style bread

In a saucepan, combine the wheat berries and water and bring to a boil. Turn the heat down to a simmer and cook the wheat berries for about an hour, or until they are soft and doubled in volume. Drain and set aside. Meanwhile, smoke the olives at 225 degrees for about an hour. In the bowl of a food processor, combine the cooked wheat berries, the smoked olives, garlic, mustard, and olive oil and blend to a paste. Serve in a crock with country-style bread. *Serves 6 to 8.*

FETTUCCINE WITH SMOKED GARLIC AND TOMATO

1 bulb fresh garlic
4 large tomatoes, cored
1/4 cup olive oil
2 pounds fettuccine
1/4 cup fresh basil, shredded
Salt and pepper to taste

Cut about 1/2-inch off the top of the whole bulb of garlic. Score tops of tomatoes and drizzle olive oil on both tomatoes and garlic. Place on a baking sheet and smoke at 225 degrees over an indirect fire for 1 hour. Cook the pasta according to package directions. While the pasta is cooking, squeeze out the garlic pulp into a bowl. Chop the tomatoes and add to garlic, along with 1/4 cup olive oil. When the pasta is done, drain it and toss with the garlic and tomato mixture. Add the fresh basil and season to taste. *Serves 6 to 8.*

FRESH FRUIT AMBROSIA WITH MINT

1 each: cantaloupe, banana, orange, and lime
1 small bunch seedless red or green grapes
1 pint strawberries, hulled
1/4 cup raisins, dark or golden
1/4 cup pecan pieces
2 tablespoons fresh mint leaves, snipped

Cube or ball the cantaloupe. Peel the banana and slice, peel the orange and lime and dice. Rinse the grapes and strawberries and slice them. Place all the cut fruit into a glass bowl and add the raisins, pecan pieces, and mint leaves. Gently toss and let stand at room temperature for about an hour to let the flavors combine. *Serves 8 to 10.*

Our thanks to Que Queen Jean Tamburello for this light and lovely ending to a meal.

LEMON BALM ICEBOX COOKIES

1 cup (2 sticks) butter
1 cup sugar
2 eggs, beaten
2 cups flour
1/2 cup finely chopped lemon balm (or substitute grated zest of 2 lemons)

Cream butter and sugar. Add eggs, flour, and lemon balm. Mix well and shape dough into 2 logs. Wrap in plastic wrap and chill for several hours. Slice cookie dough into 1/4-inch rounds. Place on a greased baking sheet for 10 to 12 minutes at 350 degrees. Cookies should just be turning brown at the edges. *Makes about 2 dozen.*

These cookies have faint green specks and are delicious served with fresh fruit or ice cream. Icebox cookies are an old-fashioned favorite for today's busy lifestyle. Que Queen Karen Adler always makes an extra batch of dough to have on hand for fresh-baked cookies in a matter of minutes. (Dough logs will keep in the freezer, wrapped in plastic wrap and packaged in a resealable plastic freezer bag, for 2 to 3 months.)

Thanksgiving Dinner, Que Queens' Style

Apple Smoked Turkey*

Rosemary Apple Salsa*

Smoky Spicy Acorn Squash*

Smoked Baked Hominy with Chile and Cheese*

Sunflower Pear Salad*

Caramelized Pumpkin Flan*

On Turkey Day (which can be any day of the year) the Que Queens give thanks for the barbecue smoker because it's directly responsible for a bird that's moist and delicious. The Queens also revel in this lighter menu that won't leave family and friends feeling stuffed and uncomfortable. With flavors so robust, no one will miss the extra fat and calories!

* RECIPE INCLUDED

APPLE-SMOKED TURKEY

1 (10 to 13-pound) turkey
1 cup balsamic vinegar
1/4 cup water
3 tablespoons paprika
2 tablespoons sea salt
2 tablespoons lemon pepper
1/4 teaspoon marjoram

Rinse turkey thoroughly and place in a large roasting pan. Combine the vinegar, water, paprika, sea salt, lemon pepper and marjoram in a glass jar, shake to blend and pour over turkey. Marinate for 1 hour or until turkey comes to room temperature, spooning marinade over the turkey several times. Build an indirect fire in a kettle grill or water smoker and add a handful of water-soaked apple wood chunks to the charcoal. Remove turkey from the marinade and place in the smoker. Smoke for 4 to 5 hours at 225 degrees until a meat thermometer inserted in the thickest part of the turkey thigh registers 170 degrees. When the turkey is smoked, the meat will have a pink color. *Serves 6 to 8.*

ROSEMARY APPLE SALSA

1 yellow bell pepper, seeded and chopped
1 Granny Smith apple, cored and chopped
1 large Jonathan apple, cored and chopped
6 green onions, chopped with part of the green
1/4 cup diced dried apricots
3 tablespoons fresh lemon juice
1/2 cup extra virgin olive oil
2 teaspoons finely chopped fresh rosemary
1/2 teaspoon sea salt
Freshly ground pepper to taste

Combine all ingredients and refrigerate one hour before serving. *Serves 6 to 8.*

SMOKY SPICY ACORN SQUASH

3 acorn squash, cut in half and seeded
3 teaspoons vegetable oil
6 tablespoons butter
2 teaspoons cinnamon
1/4 cup brown sugar
1/2 teaspoon chili powder

Brush the flesh side of each squash half with the oil. Cover each squash half with foil. Poke holes in foil to let the smoke through, and put squash, cut side down, in a 225 degree smoker for 2 hours, or until the squash is tender. Remove from smoker. Melt butter in a small skillet and add the rest of the ingredients. To serve, drizzle the spicy butter over squash half and serve. *Serves 6.*

SMOKED BAKED HOMINY WITH CHILE AND CHEESE

3 (15-ounce) cans hominy, well drained
1 clove garlic, slivered
1 small jalapeno, seeded and chopped
8 ounces Monterey Jack cheese, cubed
2 cups milk
4 eggs, beaten
1 teaspoon salt
1/4 teaspoon ground red pepper
1/2 teaspoon ground cumin

In a greased, smoke-proof baking dish, put the hominy, garlic, jalapeno, and Monterey Jack. In a small bowl, beat the milk and eggs together, then add the seasonings. Pour this mixture over the hominy. Place in a 225 degree smoker for 2 hours, or until the custard is set. *Serves 6 to 8.*

Both the squash and the hominy can be baked in a conventional oven at 350 degrees for 1 hour. But you'll miss that smoky flavor!

SUNFLOWER PEAR SALAD

2 (10-ounce) packages salad greens (or use a blend of radicchio,
escarole, frisee, leaf lettuce, etc.)
4 firm ripe pears, peeled, cored and cut into bite-sized pieces
1 tablespoon fresh lemon juice
1/2 cup raspberry vinegar
2 teaspoons Dijon mustard
1/2 cup light olive oil
2 tablespoons honey
2 tablespoons toasted sunflower seeds

Arrange the greens and the pears on salad plates. In a small bowl, whisk together the lemon juice, vinegar, mustard, olive oil, and honey. Drizzle the dressing over the pears and greens and top each salad with sunflower seeds. *Serves 6 to 8.*

CARAMELIZED PUMPKIN FLAN

2 cups sugar
2 cups canned pumpkin puree or filling
2 tablespoons butter, softened
2 cups milk
1/2 cup flour
1 teaspoon salt
1 teaspoon vanilla extract
4 eggs, beaten

Preheat the oven to 350 degrees. Put 1 cup of the sugar in the bottom of an 8-inch round aluminum cake pan. Put the cake pan on a burner over low heat and melt the sugar, slowly, until it turns a light gold. Swirl the pan to coat the bottom and sides with the caramel. Set aside on a wire rack. In a large bowl, beat the pumpkin and butter together. Blend in the milk, flour, remaining cup of sugar and rest of the ingredients. Pour the batter into the cake pan and set the pan in a large shallow baking pan containing about 1 inch of hot water. Bake for 2 hours or until a toothpick inserted in the center comes out clean. Remove pan from water and allow to cool on a wire rack. To serve, invert the cake pan onto a serving dish so that the caramel is on the top. *Serves 6 to 8.*

Hot Chicks at a Cool Soirée

Lemon Herb Smoked Chicken*

Rosemary Garlic Smoked Chicken*

Orzo and Feta Salad*

Spinach Salad with Strawberries*

Technicolor Tomatoes*

Summer Pudding*

Another dictum of the Que Queens: you can never have too much smoked chicken on hand. So we usually cook an extra one or two. We like these accompaniments, too, because they're easy, tasty and cool for a summer day. This is a great menu for a potluck salad "soirée." The hostess smokes the chicken, the guests bring the rest!

* RECIPE INCLUDED

LEMON HERB SMOKED CHICKEN

2 whole chickens (about 3 pounds each)
2 lemons
6 tablespoons Italian herb seasoning

Remove the giblets and neck from the chickens. Rinse chickens thoroughly and pat dry. Sprinkle each with the juice of 1 lemon inside and out. Place the lemon halves in the cavity of each chicken and sprinkle 1 tablespoon of the herb seasoning inside each. Rub 2 tablespoons of the seasoning on the outside of each bird. Smoke over an indirect charcoal fire topped with water-soaked mesquite or pecan wood chunks at 225 degrees for 2-1/2 hours. Chicken is done when the leg joint moves easily. *Serves 4 to 6.*

ROSEMARY GARLIC SMOKED CHICKEN

2 whole chickens (about 3 pounds each)
2 tablespoons olive oil
2 tablespoons chopped rosemary
2 bulbs fresh garlic

Remove the giblets and neck from the chickens. Rinse chickens thoroughly and pat dry. Rub 1 tablespoon olive oil over each chicken and rub in 1 tablespoon rosemary. Cut about 1/2-inch off the top of each garlic bulb and place a bulb in the cavity of each chicken. Smoke over an indirect charcoal fire topped with water-soaked mesquite and apple wood chunks at 225 degrees for 2-1/2 hours. Chicken is done when the leg joint moves easily. *Serves 4 to 6.*

When you do as the Queens do and cook an extra chick or two, you'll be able to create truly lovely leftovers. Try adding chicken to salads or chowders, topping baked potatoes, combining with black beans and corn in a casserole, blending with cream cheese and ancho chile for a dip. The possibilities are practically endless!

ORZO AND FETA SALAD

1/2 pound orzo, cooked
1/2 cup chopped green onion
1/2 cup crumbled feta cheese
1/3 cup olive oil
3 tablespoons fresh lemon juice
1 tablespoon fresh dill (or 1 teaspoon dried)
1/4 teaspoon dried oregano
Salt and freshly ground pepper to taste

In a large bowl, combine the orzo, onion, and feta. In a small bowl, whisk together the oil, lemon juice, and seasonings. Pour the dressing over the orzo and toss to blend. Refrigerate until ready to serve. *Serves 4 to 6.*

SPINACH SALAD WITH STRAWBERRIES

6 cups torn fresh spinach
3 cups sliced strawberries
3/4 cup sliced green onions
4-1/2 tablespoons fresh orange juice
3 tablespoons balsamic vinegar
1 tablespoon olive oil
1-1/2 tablespoons sesame seeds, toasted

Combine the first 3 ingredients in a large bowl. Whisk together the orange juice, vinegar, and olive oil and drizzle over the salad. Toss gently to blend. Arrange salad on plates and sprinkle with toasted sesame seeds. *Serves 4 to 6.*

TECHNICOLOR TOMATOES

4 to 6 large fresh tomatoes, preferably a mix of colors
1 red onion, sliced thinly
1 cup cider vinegar
2 to 4 tablespoons sugar
1/4 cup chopped Italian parsley

Slice the tomatoes and arrange on a platter. Top with the onion. Add sugar to the vinegar and adjust the sweetness to your taste. Drizzle the sauce over the tomatoes and garnish with the parsley. *Serves 4 to 6.*

SUMMER PUDDING

6 to 8 slices good-quality stale bread, crusts removed
3 pints fresh or frozen mixed berries (blackberries, blueberries, strawberries, etc.)
1/4 cup sugar or to taste
Lemon juice to taste
Whipped cream, ice cream or frozen yogurt to garnish

The night before serving, cut the bread to fit the top, bottom, and sides of a medium to small mixing bowl. Cook the fruit and sugar in a saucepan over medium heat until the mixture begins to boil. Remove from heat, add lemon juice, and taste. If necessary, add more sugar. Pour the fruit into the bread-lined bowl and top with the bread "lid." Set a plate on top of the bread lid and place a heavy can on top of the plate to weight it down. Refrigerate overnight. The pudding is ready when the juice has permeated the bread and turned it a purplish color. To serve, invert the pudding on a plate. Serve each wedge of pudding with whipped cream, ice cream or frozen yogurt. *Serves 6 to 8.*

Pigging Out the "New-Fashioned" Way

Peppered Pork Roast*

Cherry Salsa*

Snow Peas with Julienne Bell Peppers*

Smoked Baked Sweet Potatoes*

Mixed Greens with Radicchio

Wildflower Honey Creams with
Summer Berries*

When the Que Queens pig out, we do it in style. We may not use finger bowls, but the feast is just as royal. Our succulent pork roast always makes our subjects happy. We're sure your group will feel they've dined in high style. And wait until they try these sweet potatoes!

* RECIPE INCLUDED

PEPPERED PORK ROAST

3 pound boneless pork loin roast
2 tablespoons freshly ground black pepper
2 teaspoons garlic salt
Apple juice for basting

Prepare smoker for 225 degree indirect cooking. Place water-soaked cherry or apple wood chunks over the charcoal. Fill a water pan and place in the smoker. Rub pepper and garlic salt into pork roast covering all surfaces. Place pork roast in the smoker and cook indirect for 1/2 hour. Turn the roast and brush it with apple juice and cook for 1-1/2 more hours, basting every 20 minutes, until internal temperature reaches 155 to 160 degrees. Remove roast from the grill, cover with plastic wrap and let stand for 10 minutes. Then slice and serve with Cherry Salsa. *Serves 6 to 8.*

CHERRY SALSA

1/3 cup chopped onion
1/3 cup chopped green pepper
1/3 cup chopped green chilies
1/3 cup dried cherries, chopped
1/3 cup red cherry jam
1-1/2 tablespoons vinegar
1-1/2 tablespoons chopped cilantro

Combine all ingredients and mix well. Cover and chill several hours or overnight. *Makes 2 cups.*

The Peppered Pork Roast and Cherry Salsa recipes are courtesy of the National Pork Producers Council. The Que Queens have adapted it for the smoker!

SNOW PEAS WITH JULIENNE BELL PEPPERS

1/2 pound snow peas
1 red bell pepper, julienned
1 yellow bell pepper, julienned
1 orange bell pepper, julienned
2 tablespoons butter
Seasoned salt to taste

Rinse and dry vegetables. Sauté in butter until tender crisp, about 6 to 8 minutes. Season with salt. *Serves 6 to 8.*

SMOKED BAKED SWEET POTATOES

6 to 8 sweet potatoes
Vegetable oil
Salt, pepper, and butter to taste

Scrub potatoes and prick with a roasting fork. Rub with vegetable oil. Smoke over indirect heat for 2 hours at 225 degrees or until potatoes are done. To serve, split potatoes and season to taste. *Serves 6 to 8.*

Whipped honey butter adds a slightly sweet flavor to these smoky, velvety potatoes.

WILDFLOWER HONEY CREAMS WITH SUMMER BERRIES

1 cup heavy cream
1 cup sour cream
3/4 cup wildflower honey (or use a darker honey)
6 cups fresh or frozen berries (blackberries, blueberries, raspberries)
Juice of 1 lemon
1 teaspoon ground cinnamon

In a medium bowl, whip the cream until it makes stiff peaks. Blend in the sour cream and 1/4 cup of wildflower honey and set aside. In a large saucepan heat the berries, the remaining 1/2 cup of honey, lemon juice and cinnamon until the berries come to a simmer. Remove from heat and let cool slightly. Portion out the berries into 6 bowls and top with the honey cream. *Serves 6 to 8.*

This recipe was created by Que Queen Judith Fertig and appeared in her award-winning cookbook,"Pure Prairie, Farm Fresh and Wildly Delicious Foods From the Prairie." It's a delightful finale to any good meal.

Another dessert option, for heartier appetites, comes from Que Queen Becky Baker. Becky says this "fruity dump cake" can be put together in less than 3 minutes. In a greased and floured 9-inch x 13-inch cake pan, pour each of the following ingredients in order listed, spreading evenly to cover pan:

1 (15-ounce) can crushed pineapple, undrained
1 (15-ounce) can cherry pie filling
1 box yellow cake mix
1/2 cup chopped nuts
1-1/2 sticks margarine (cut into pats)

Bake at 350 degrees for 1 hour.

Fishing for Compliments

Smoked Salmon with Vermouth and Lemon*

Mixed Greens with Smoked Goat Cheese*

New Potato Salad with Wasabi Mayonnaise*

Warm French Bread

Raspberry Fool *

Almond Cookie Brittle*

A cool meal for a warm evening and perfect with a crisp chablis or tart chardonnay. Simple, yet sophisticated, this menu is just right for an "al fresco" dinner or a more formal "linen tablecloth" occasion indoors.

* RECIPE INCLUDED

SMOKED SALMON WITH VERMOUTH AND LEMON

1 (3 to 4-pound) salmon, cleaned and dressed
1 lemon, sliced
6 fresh dill sprigs
1/2 cup dry vermouth
1/4 cup fresh lemon juice
3 tablespoons butter, melted
1 clove garlic, minced

Prepare an indirect fire of water-soaked alder or grape wood over charcoal. Place lemon slices and sprigs of dill in the cavity of the salmon. Set aside. Put the rest of the ingredients in a saucepan and bring to the boil, then set aside. Place the salmon on top of a piece of heavy duty foil large enough to enclose the salmon. Crimp 3 sides to hold the baste (the other side will fold over). Pour the baste over salmon, fold over the foil to enclose the salmon and crimp the edges together. Smoke at 225 degrees for 1 hour. Open the foil, but make sure edges stay crimped to hold in the baste. Smoke for 1 more hour, or until fish flakes easily with a fork. *Serves 4 to 6.*

Leftover salmon, combined with leftover potato salad, makes a delightful lunch or supper dish. And the salmon, combined with cream cheese and seasoned with a little lemon juice and Worcestershire sauce, makes a delicious paté to serve with water crackers.

MIXED GREENS WITH SMOKED GOAT CHEESE

1/4 cup olive oil
1/4 teaspoon each salt and pepper
1/3 cup toasted bread crumbs
4 (3-ounce) portions fresh goat cheese
1 (10-ounce) package European salad greens (or a mix of your choice)
1 cup cherry tomatoes
1 cup bottled vinaigrette dressing

In a small bowl, blend the olive oil, salt and pepper. Put the bread crumbs on a separate dish. Dip each portion of cheese in the olive oil mixture, then the bread crumbs. Place on a baking tray and smoke over an indirect fire for 1 hour. Place each piece of goat cheese on a bed of greens and drizzle with vinaigrette. *Serves 4.*

NEW POTATO SALAD WITH WASABI MAYONNAISE

1-1/2 pounds new potatoes, scrubbed
2 tablespoons chopped green onion
1 carrot, peeled and shredded
1 cup good-quality mayonnaise
1 tablespoon wasabi powder (Japanese horseradish, available at gourmet markets)

Place unpeeled potatoes in a large pot and cover with water. Bring to a boil and cook for 15 minutes, or until the potatoes are tender. Drain and let cool. In a large bowl, blend the other ingredients together. Add the cooked potatoes and toss to cover. Cover and chill until ready to serve. *Serves 4 to 6.*

RASPBERRY FOOL

1-1/2 cups fresh raspberries
1 tablespoon sugar, or more to taste
1-1/4 cups heavy cream
Mint or lemon balm leaves to garnish

Reserve a few perfect berries for decoration. Put the remaining berries and the sugar in a bowl and mash with a potato masher (do not use a food processor because the texture will be too fine). Whip the cream until stiff. Fold the berry mixture into the cream. Pour the fool into 4 dessert cups or glasses, cover and chill until ready to serve. Garnish each dessert with fresh berries and a mint leaf and serve with Almond Cookie Brittle. *Serves 4.*

Fruit fools have been a popular dessert in England for hundreds of years. One explanation of the name is that it came about because "any fool could make this dish."

ALMOND COOKIE BRITTLE

1 cup (2 sticks) butter or margarine, softened
1 cup sugar
1 teaspoon salt
1-1/2 teaspoons almond extract
2 cups all-purpose flour
1 cup sliced almonds

Preheat oven to 350 degrees. Combine butter, sugar, salt, and almond extract, and beat until creamy. Stir in flour gradually, beating until blended. Fold in nuts, then press dough into a jelly-roll pan. Bake for 20 to 25 minutes (the shorter time it bakes, the chewier it stays; longer baking produces a crisper cookie). Leave in pan to cool, then break apart like peanut brittle. Store in an airtight container. *Makes about 2 dozen pieces.*

This crunchy cookie recipe came from Honorary Que Queen Richie Cusick. She also makes a chocolate chip version. Replace the almond extract with vanilla extract, use walnuts or pecans in place of almonds and add 1 cup chocolate chips! A royal thank you to Richie!

The Long-Live-the-Queens Birthday Brunch

Royal Slush*

Smoky Spicy Nuts*

Smoked Apricot Ham*

Asparagus and Cheese Frittata*

Caramel Apple Muffins*

Easy Royal Rumtopf*

When England celebrates the Queen's birthday, there's a parade. When the Que Queens celebrate a birthday, there's a barbecue. Of course! To toast one of our own, we brew up a batch of Royal Slush and go whole hog (so to speak)—actually, whole ham. Here's our celebration brunch menu with a little something for everyone—sweet and savory, sour and salty, hot and cold. And all good!

* RECIPE INCLUDED

SMOKED APRICOT HAM

1 (5 to 7-pound) bone-in ham (shank or butt)
2 cups apricot preserves
2-1/2 teaspoons dry mustard
1-1/2 tablespoons cider vinegar
20 cloves

Prepare an indirect fire adding water-soaked cherry and oak chips to the charcoal. Remove the thick outer skin of the ham, score the fat, and stud the ham with cloves. Combine the apricot preserves, mustard, and vinegar and coat the ham. Let stand 1 hour to marinate. Reserve any leftover glaze. Smoke ham for 2 to 3 hours at 225 degrees. Baste with glaze 2 or 3 times while smoking. *Serves 10 to 12.*

Quick Apricot Chutney goes well with the ham. (See page 27 for recipe.)

ROYAL SLUSH

7 cups water
5 green tea bags
1-1/2 cups sugar
1 (12-ounce) can orange juice, thawed
1 (12-ounce) can lemonade, thawed
2 cups apricot brandy

Bring the water to a boil, remove from the heat, stir in the sugar and plunge in the tea bags. Let steep for 2 hours. Remove the tea bags and transfer the tea to a large metal mixing bowl. Add the orange juice, lemonade, and apricot brandy and stir well. Freeze, covered, for at least 24 hours. To serve, scoop several cups into the blender, blend and serve in glasses. Makes 12 cups.

Que Queen Bobbi Marks contributed the formula for this royal beverage. Thanks, Bobbi!

SMOKY SPICY NUTS

3 teaspoons curry powder
1/4 cup Worcestershire sauce
1/2 cup water
2 teaspoons sugar
2 garlic cloves, minced
1 teaspoon salt
4 cups whole, shelled almonds

Combine the marinade ingredients in a bowl. Add almonds and marinate for an hour. Drain the nuts and place on a greased cookie sheet in a single layer. Smoke in a 225 degree smoker for 1 hour, or until the nuts are crisp and lightly smoked. Serve immediately or store in a covered container. *Serves 12.*

Honorary Que Queen, Dee Barwick, suggests making a double batch of these flavorful nuts. They are a great appetizer (especially with a glass of Royal Slush). Keep some on hand to treat unexpected guests. Plus, they make a welcome gift on any occasion!

ASPARAGUS AND CHEESE FRITTATA

1/4 cup olive oil
2 yellow onions, peeled and sliced thinly
1 pound asparagus, trimmed and cooked until crisp/tender
1 cup grated Gruyere cheese
2 tablespoons chopped parsley
A dozen eggs, beaten

Preheat oven to 450 degrees. Pour the oil in a large baking dish and arrange the onion slices on bottom of dish. Bake for 5 minutes, then remove dish from oven and reduce heat to 400 degrees. Cut the asparagus on the diagonal into 1-inch pieces. Sprinkle the asparagus over the onion, then top with the cheese and parsley. Pour the beaten eggs over the vegetables and cheese. Bake for 20 minutes, or until the frittata has puffed and browned and the center of the omelet is set. Do not over cook. Serve in wedges, hot or at room temperature. *Serves 12.*

CARAMEL APPLE MUFFINS

1-1/2 cups brown sugar
2/3 cup oil
1 egg, beaten
1 cup buttermilk
1 teaspoon baking soda
1 teaspoon salt
1 teaspoon vanilla
2-1/2 cups all-purpose flour
1-1/2 cups diced apples
1/2 cup chopped pecans
1 dozen soft caramel candies
1 tablespoon butter, softened
1/3 cup granulated sugar

Preheat the oven to 325 degrees. Combine brown sugar, oil and egg. In another bowl combine buttermilk, soda, salt and vanilla. Add this mixture to sugar mixture and alternate with flour. Mix well after each addition. Fold in diced apples and chopped pecans. Pour into muffin tins and press 1 caramel candy into each muffin. Sprinkle with 1/3 cup sugar combined with 1 tablespoon butter. Bake for 30 minutes. *Makes 2 dozen.*

EASY ROYAL RUMTOPF

2 pounds mixed dried fruit
1 cup dark rum
4 cups water
1 cup sugar
2 cups whipped topping (optional)

Combine all ingredients in a saucepan and simmer until tender, about 30 minutes. Add more water, if necessary. "Crown" with a dollop of whipped topping. *Serves 12.*

RECIPE INDEX

RECIPE INDEX

RECIPE INDEX

ABOUT THE AUTHORS

Karen Adler started the publishing firm of Pig Out Publications, Inc. in 1988, launching a line of successful barbecue and grilling cookbooks that includes *Barbecue Greats Memphis Style, Texas Barbecue, Wild About Kansas City Barbecue, Bar-B-Que Barbecue Barbeque, Bar-B-Q B-B-Q*, and *Vegetables on the Grill*. Her company is the largest supplier of books on the subject of outdoor cooking in the world. She is author/publisher of *Hooked on Fish on the Grill* and *Barbecued Ribs-Rubbed, Glazed & Sauced*. She is also author of the *Best Little Grilling Cookbook, Best Little Barbecue Cookbook, Best Little Marinades Cookbook*, and the *Best Little BBQ Sauces Cookbook* (Celestial Arts, Ten Speed Press, Berkeley, California). Karen is an accomplished cook, and has taught cooking classes at Halls of Kansas City, the Kitchen Conservatory in St. Louis, Cooks of Crocus Hill in Minneapolis/St. Paul, and is a regular instructor at the Culinary Center of Kansas City. Her barbecue related activities include membership in the National Barbecue Association (NBBQA) and the Kansas City Barbecue Society. She writes the book review column for Barbecue Today. Karen is a graduate of the Greasehouse University and holds the prestigious M.B. (Master of Barbecue) degree and is founder of the BBQ Queens.

Award-winning food writer and cookbook author Judith Fertig is a barbecue convert. Orginally from Cincinnati where folks bake or boil ribs before grilling (shocking!), she has now seen the light. . . when the smoke doesn't get in her eyes. Her work has appeared internationally in publications such as Saveur, Country Home, On the Grill, Country Living, USAir, The New York Times, The London Sunday Times, The San Francisco Chronicle, and The Kansas City Star. She is author of the award-winning cookbook *Pure Prairie – Farm Fresh and Wildly Delicious Foods from the Prairie* (1996, Two Lane Press) and James Beard Award Nominee for *Prairie Home Cooking* (1999, Harvard Common Press). Judith is a founding member of the Kansas City chapter of the American Institute of Wine and Food, the International Association of Culinary Professionals, and the Kansas City Barbeque Society. Judith and Karen are also founding members of the Kansas City Chapter of Les Dames d' Escoffier. Judith has studied at the Cordon Bleu in London and La Varenne in Paris. She enjoys being a BBQ Queen, and tries to add to her stash of tiaras whenever she can.

BOOKS ON BARBECUE

The popularity of cookbooks available for the grill and barbecue enthusiasts is ever growing. Here is a list of favorites, some old and some new. For a complete list of over 200 titles on outdoor cooking visit www.pigoutpublications.com.

Barbecue America by Rick Browne & Jack Bettridge (1999, Time Life Books)

Barbecue Bible by Steven Raichlen (1998, Workman Publishing)

Barbecue Greats Memphis Style by Carolyn Wells (1992, Pig Out Publications)

Barbecue Inferno by Dave DeWitt (2001, Ten Speed Press)

Barbecued Ribs-Rubbed, Sauced & Glazed by Karen Adler (2001, Pig Out Publications)

Barbecuing & Sausage Making Secrets by Charlie and Ruthie Knote (1993, Culinary Institute of Smoke Cooking)

Best Little Barbecue Cookbook by Karen Adler (1999, Ten Speed Press)

Best Little BBQ Sauces Cookbook by Karen Adler (1999, Ten Speed Press)

Best Little Grilling Cookbook by Karen Adler (1999, Ten Speed Press)

Best Little Marinades Cookbook by Karen Adler (1999, Ten Speed Press)

Cooking with Fire and Smoke by Phillip Stephen Schulz (1986, Simon & Schuster)

Easy Grilling & Simple Smoking by the BBQ Queens Karen Adler & Judith Fertig (1997, 2001 Pig Out Publications)

Great BBQ Sauce Book by Ardie Davis (1999, Ten Speed Press)

Great Ribs Book by Hugh Carpenter and Teri Sandison (1999, Ten Speed Press)

Grilling Encyclopedia by A. Cort Sinnes (1992, Atlantic Monthly Press)

Hooked on Fish on the Grill by Karen Adler (1992, Pig Out Publications)

Hot Barbecue! by Hugh Carpenter and Teri Sandison (1996, Ten Speed Press)

Kansas City Barbeque Society Cookbook (1996, Kansas City Barbeque Society)

Smoke & Spice by Cheryl and Bill Jamison (1994, Harvard Common Press)

Sublime Smoke by Cheryl and Bill Jamison (1996, Harvard Common Press)

Vegetables on the Grill by Shifra Stein (1998, Pig Out Publications)

Wild About Kansas City Barbecue by Rich Davis and Shifra Stein (2000, Pig Out Publications)